Growing Up has NEVER been easy...

by Charles Acrie Jr.

"Especially when you make it hard on yourself."

outskirtspress
DENVER, COLORADO

The opinions expressed in this manuscript are solely the opinions of the author and do not represent the opinions or thoughts of the publisher. The author has represented and warranted full ownership and/or legal right to publish all the materials in this book.

Growing Up Has Never Been Easy...
Especially When You Make It Hard On Yourself
All Rights Reserved.
Copyright © 2015 Charles Acrie Jr.
v2.0

Cover Photo © 2015 Carlos St. Mary. All rights reserved - used with permission.

This book may not be reproduced, transmitted, or stored in whole or in part by any means, including graphic, electronic, or mechanical without the express written consent of the publisher except in the case of brief quotations embodied in critical articles and reviews.

Outskirts Press, Inc.
http://www.outskirtspress.com

ISBN: 978-1-4787-6092-4

Outskirts Press and the "OP" logo are trademarks belonging to Outskirts Press, Inc.

PRINTED IN THE UNITED STATES OF AMERICA

Table of Contents

PROLOGUE i
FAMILY BUSINESS 1
UNEDUCATED FOOL 11
BULLY ME NOT! 17
SPORTS AND ACADEMICS 25
TO BANG OR NOT TO BANG 31
DRUGGED OUT 42
POOR CHOICES COULD MEAN JAIL/PRISON 56
A LEADER OF MEN 85
DOGG POUND DREAMING 91
MY TURNAROUND 102
EPILOGUE 112

PROLOGUE

My name is Charles Eugene Acrie Jr. and I'm the president of The Heal Through Laughter Foundation, a nonprofit 501(c)(3) corporation that utilizes the method of laughter to bring about joy and happiness where people have a difficult time finding it. I had to overcome incredible odds to get to where I am today. If I had to do it all over again, would I do it differently? Of course I would.

I'm writing this book to assist people, both young and old, and educate them about the process of decision-making and how making poor choices can alter the course of your life in the most tragic of ways. Most of the mistakes we make during the course of our lives are based on poor decision-making. During the course of my life, I made one bad decision after another. I don't have all of these horrible stories of abuse; most of my troubles were self-induced.

You know it's crazy, because when you are a child, there is just so much you don't understand when it comes to your parents and the day-to-day decisions they have to make. You don't really understand the grind, and in most cases you really don't care until you become grown and have your own children and responsibilities.

I don't know why I continued to fail all of my life, or why I couldn't seem to complete anything. The last thing I can remember actually completing—before my transformation, of course—was my elementary graduation.

I didn't graduate from junior high school; I got kicked out of the school district. I didn't graduate from high school. Despite being a standout basketball player with major college offers from around the United States, I didn't have enough credits to graduate. I went to a junior college, but I didn't graduate from there either.

Who does this? How does that happen? How does a student get through school, literally failing, and no one seem the wiser? Those answers and more will be revealed as we get into *Growing Up Has Never Been Easy*.

Well, I can't say that I didn't complete anything before my transformation—the state and the federal government made damn sure I completed each one of my prison sentences. I have served time in the city, county, state and the feds—and for what? I had every opportunity in the world to succeed. What kept me from achieving my fullest potential? What kept me going back and forth, in and out of jail? There were many reasons, but at the forefront of my problems was my failure to make the right choices.

During the course of my life, I made excuses for my inability to achieve. I had to because my underachieving was such an embarrassment that I could barely face myself, let alone other people who recognized my obvious abilities and talents.

For a long time, I blamed my father for my problems. Sure, he could have been a better father to me, but he was a better father to me than I had been to my children. I could have been a better son. Although my father and I never really connected as father and son, he made sure I had what I needed. I lived with him while I was in high school and I never lived up to his reasonable expectations.

My father was a human resource administrator. I say *was* because he's now retired and living off the fruit of his labor. I used to always tell myself that I would never be like him. In many ways, if I were more like my father I would have grown up a much better person. The one thing I didn't take from him was his work ethic.

I was good at many things but never great at anything, not even crime, because obviously I kept getting caught. I never really held a job because the jobs I was qualified for I thought I was too good for, and the jobs I wanted were too good for me.

One of the worst days of my life was when my mother died in 2005. My mother died without me doing what I always wanted to do for her, and that was to set her up in a house that I bought for her. My mother died without having that feeling of pride for her eldest child, her son. She did all she could for my sister, brother, and I. She was a really hard worker, and better than that, she was a brilliant artist. She died well before her time. Man, I really miss her.

I guess the best way to describe me is the ultimate underachiever. My abilities far exceeded my accomplishments. I never wanted to work hard, but wanted to take the easiest road toward what I thought success was; in the process I made one bad decision after another. I've made so many mistakes in my life. A great many people had to suffer, including my children, my now ex-wife, people with whom I had various other relationships, and my family.

That is the reason I'm writing this book, because I find myself in the unique position to educate people based on all of the poor decisions and mistakes that I've made. I was even a crackhead! Can you believe it? I had been smoking weed from the age of eleven. When I turned 13, I experimented with angel dust, or sherm, and from there I tried powder cocaine and speed. When affordable cocaine "found it's way into the hood," crack was the thing.

When I was in federal prison, I had counseling just to reduce my sentence. I wasn't trying to get well—I was trying get out of prison early! I figured since I was there, I might as well participate. I took that time to honestly breakdown the person I really was, separating my true self from the self I manufactured or made my representative.

I didn't like what I saw and it really hurt me. I always thought my problems had started around junior high school, but found out things actually started much earlier.

I was so amazed at what I discovered about myself. After I got over the shock, all I wanted to do was get better. I didn't know what to do to get better, but I knew I needed to make wiser decisions to cut down on my mistakes. I knew I had to make healthier decisions on everything I did—not just the big things, but everything.

I've never heard of a book where the credibility of the author is the fact that he failed at everything. There are two kinds of people who have the credibility to give advice: 1) the person who has succeeded at everything or 2) the person who has failed at everything.

Most people, especially kids, don't want to hear what a person has to say who has succeeded at everything because they feel that person has nothing in common with what they have to endure on a day-to-day basis. But what excuse do you give a person who has failed at everything and has overcome those failures?

I guess that's what makes my situation unique. I was able to dissect myself, breaking everything down to the lowest form, and then rebuild myself. Most people don't ever figure out their problems, never mind being able to fix them.

I've made more mistakes as an adult than I ever had as a child. At least as a child I could blame my ignorance on my youth. As an adult, making the same mistakes over and over again makes me look retarded. How else would you explain it? Some call it insanity.

Growing Up Has Never Been Easy is a straight-talk guide, a pull-no-punches book toward bridging the gap between parent and child and furthering the understanding of self, family, childhood, adulthood, and parenthood.

This is a book written by a man who has made every conceivable mistake any one human being can make, but who has been able to make the necessary corrections to become a successful member of society. I have written this book so that young kids, as well as their parents, can avoid making these same mistakes. I want them to know they are not alone and there are solutions.

Growing Up Has Never Been Easy: Especially When You Make It Hard On Yourself will mean prevention for some, and correction for others. Whatever the case, we want to get back to old-fashioned values, where men are raising their children and providing for their households as head of their families. We want to get back to husbands and wives working together, children obeying their parents and learning from their mistakes, mothers teaching their daughters how to be responsible women, fathers teaching their sons to be responsible men, parents nurturing their children, and children looking after and loving each other.

FAMILY BUSINESS

When it comes to living a productive life or trying to make corrections to your existing life, home and family are the places to start. We can all agree that every family and every household is different. Some homes have both parents in them, and many only have one parent in them. Some of you may live with an extended family other than your parents.

When I was growing up, in my early beginning, my father and mother were together. My father was a military man and my mother was an administrative assistant. Those years were a bit foggy. All I can remember was that we were living in North Dakota for a bit, and then California for a bit. Then the next thing I knew we were living in Gary, Indiana, with my grandparents in the projects and my father was not there.

I really wasn't sure why he wasn't there and it didn't bother me much because I knew my mother would be there. I was a real boy. I loved to go outside and I loved sports.

For a time we lived with my grandmother and grandfather in Gary, Indiana. My grandfather worked in the steel mill. I was only about six years old and I didn't understand how difficult it was working in the steel mill. I just always went along with the program. He also used to box and would teach me a few boxing moves.

My grandmother didn't work but took care of the household. I really enjoyed those times. My mother worked, though. She had amazing office skills and she would catch the train to Chicago every morning, five days a week.

Even though my mother and grandfather worked, we saw many hungry times. Sometimes we would have so little food that we would have to go to bed before the sun went down. I remember my sister and I would peep through the curtains and watch the kids play while lying in the bed. We were hungry and couldn't go outside to play. I think not being able to play with the other kids hurt more than not having anything to eat.

I was a really active kid. I would get whippings often. Back in those days we were forced to get our own switches from the tree. As a kid, you would get the littlest switch you could find, and then my grandmother would send my Aunt Debra to get the kind of switch she wanted. My aunt would get a switch that could be used for firewood after my grandmother was finished whipping me (just kidding, but not much).

I used to get Hot Wheels with the racetrack for Christmas and I would love it—until I realized that it was a setup, because the Hot Wheels were not just for me. After I would have a nice little time with my Hot Wheels, I would get whippings with the little orange tracks when I did something wrong. Didn't like the Hot Wheels much after that.

We finally moved from my grandparent's home and moved into a place down the street from the Jacksons. I played with them sometimes but didn't really know who they were until we moved.

We eventually moved to Carson, California, from Indiana. We met up with my father and for a minute we were one little happy family.

My father and mother bought a three-bedroom house in Carson,

California. Carson was a rising community of middle-class people. My sister and I had our own rooms, which was quite different from where we had lived in Gary.

For some reason there was a disconnection between my father and me. He seemed extremely mean to me and I wasn't really comfortable around him. He was much nicer to my sister—you know, daddy's little girl. I don't know how much the closeness they shared affected me. I believed that as long as his attention was on her he didn't have time to fuss at me, and I was good with that.

As I reflect back on things, my father and I were both uncomfortable around each other. He wasn't the affectionate kind of father who held me and told me that he loved me. I'm not sure if it was the time he spent away in the military or because he and my mother separated that kept us from being as close as we could have been. All I know is that it was what it was.

My father wasn't a bad man; as a matter of fact, he was a good man. He took me fishing; we went out to the park to play basketball and things like that. I don't remember us communicating very much. I think he had expectations of me that I wasn't living up to. Now that's only speculation regarding when I was a child, but I know that was the case as I got older.

Carson, California, was really a nice place to live. On the surface we appeared to be the perfect family, but what was happening underneath was turmoil. My father was a player. He loved the women and the women loved him.

One day my father went on a weekend fishing trip. When he got home he was in his fishing outfit and he handed my mother some fish to clean. He came in shivering, saying, "Ahhhhh man, it was cold out there," as he motioned to my mother to clean the fish.

My mother took the fish and began to clean them when she stopped abruptly. She left the house and went to the driveway and checked inside the car and then she checked the trunk. In the trunk, my father had his dress clothes and other things that led my mother to believe he didn't go fishing after all.

My mother came back into the house and began to wail on my father. He tried to control her and finally threw her on the bed and jumped on top of her, and I jumped on top of him. My sister was crying, my mother was frantic, and I was in attack mode.

I was only about eleven, and clearly no match for my father. My father began to pound on what I thought was my mother's face, but he was actually pounding the pillow next to her face. My father is not a violent man, but he knew he had been caught and I guess he was trying to scare her.

You are probably wondering why my mother just stopped cleaning fish so abruptly and went to the car. No, she didn't have special powers. What happened was, as she cleaned the fish, she noticed that a stamp on the side of the fish read "Joe's Fish Market"!

Sorry, dad, I had to tell that story. As sad as that story was back then, it is hilarious today!

That was the end of their marriage. I don't think they were in love anymore and my father left us with the house. I can't say I was really that sad, because my father and I were still worlds apart when it came to closeness. In some ways, I felt free.

When my parents separated it didn't dawn on me that financially this would hurt my mother. She was working at TRW Aerospace at the time, and was now a single parent, but she had a mortgage, bills, kids, and not to mention the emotional turmoil she had to endure by being separated from her husband. I'm pretty sure that for a time my father assisted her with the bills; after all, his name was on them as well.

As a kid, the only thing that changed for me was that my father was gone, but I expected things to be exactly the way they always had been. I expected the lights to stay on, to continue to have a roof over my head, to have food in the refrigerator, and to continue receiving the clothes and shoes I wanted.

My mother was the kind of person who didn't want to hear anything bad. She never wanted to discuss anything negative, and in some ways I became the same way. This is how I was in school. My mother had to be having a difficult time as I reflect back on the situation as an adult.

There was a little boy, Reggie Landry, who moved around the corner from me, and he became my best friend. I didn't have kids who I could actually call my friends. He was my best friend until the day he died at age nineteen. He was shot in the chest while another friend was robbing this old man, because he was broke. Reggie was sitting on the car when our friend came running around the corner, being chased and shot at by the old man. Reggie took a bullet in the chest. That was my boy.

My mother finally met someone—another Charles. It seemed that my mother had a thing for men named Charles. He had been married before and had kids. They eventually got married and had a son, Sterling. My mother loved her husband until his death. I think she died because she may have missed him so much. To this day his kids are still family to me and I love them dearly.

I told a story about my father, so it is only fair that I give you one about my mother. Once, when I got home from school, I began to look around my mother and Charles's bedroom. Back then I had a habit of snooping.

Anyway, I'm looking around and I decided to go in between the mattress and box springs of their bed to see what I could find. I found some pictures, and for a moment I really didn't recognize the images I saw, then it hit me. They were pictures of my mother naked. I almost fainted.

I began to gag, because it tripped me out seeing my mother in that way. I never, ever, ever, ever, ever told her what I saw, and it was very difficult for me to look my mother directly in the face after that. Even as I sit here reflecting back on that day I feel like gagging. I never, ever, ever, ever, ever snooped in my mother's room again. Sorry, mom.

Bringing someone into your household is a tricky situation. The love and the idea of love sometimes conflict with the practicality of running a family. Sometimes the person you bring in is not ready for that type of commitment, but enjoys the security that the relationship may bring.

In my relationships I always went in with great intentions, but somehow I always messed things up. I got along with the kids because I was a big kid myself. It was the responsibilities that I fell short on. Whether I was out there hustling backward, on drugs, or in jail, it was all a waste of time.

I was trying to get myself together while the children suffered. I put them in the same position that I went through, but different. I didn't teach them work ethics because I had none. I didn't teach them what a good father was because I wasn't one. I didn't teach them what a good spouse was supposed to be because I wasn't one.

When I think about it, I wasn't really taught anything myself, so how could I teach anything to anybody? I was always so good at covering up my flaws that everyone thought I was okay. I wasn't okay.

As a child, things happen around you that you know nothing about, but it can affect and dictate your thought process and the outcome of your life. Take the decisions your parents make, for instance. In my day, children were told to be seen and not heard, or people would tell you to, "Do what I say, not what I do."

A child is going to do exactly what he or she sees the parents do, whether the parents like it or not. With the knowledge and information kids of today have, I don't know how they would have made it back in my day. Well, I guess the parents of my era thought the same thing about us.

As grownups, we don't really think the things we do could affect the lives of our children. We are so busy caught up in our own struggles or selfishness that we lose sight of the children. Now I know it isn't easy trying to work, run the household, squeeze in some "you" time, and pay full attention to your children, but it is extremely important as a parent to make the time.

I'm not the most spiritual person in the world, but there are some scriptures in the Bible that are essential to raising a child. Proverbs 22:6 says, "Train up a child in the way that they should go, and when they grow old they will not depart from it." This is the one that I feel most connected to.

There is nothing more important than family. Sometimes we put value on things and people who are not our family and we become led astray. Family and home is your safe haven as long as it is a healthy environment. It takes the entire family to work on making home and family what it is supposed to be: loving.

To the Parents:

We by nature are creatures of habit—that's why we have to catch the kids when they are young. If there are both parents in the household, both parents need to share in that responsibility. If there is one person in the household, then that parent has to work twice as hard.

Never take for granted that your spouse is doing the things for the children that you yourself should and could be doing. Single parents, don't take for granted that your child is doing the things you think they should be doing just because you don't **SEE** anything wrong. Train your children to do the things you know they should be doing. Stay in your children's business!

If you are a single parent, be careful whom you let in your household. The two of you must be on the same page or there will be a problem. If that person you bring into your household does not increase the family's quality of life, **JUST SAY NO!**

Kids are a great deal smarter than we were when we were growing up. These are **CYBER KIDS!** They are smarter and have more access to more technology and information than we could ever have imagined at our age growing up. You have to basically have a college degree to keep up with your own children these days. Don't let the computer raise your child.

The way social media is today, you have to make sure your children are doing what they are supposed to be doing. You have to monitor them, because if you don't, someone else online may be monitoring them.

When I got bad grades I would just forge my mother's signature and keep it moving. These days, when children get a bad grade and don't want their parents to find out, they have the capability of hacking into the school computers to change their grades to the grades they desire. Is that crazy or what? That is the reason to train the children as early as possible so there would be no need for them to cheat.

For the most part, the game between parent and child is a complex one. The child is constantly trying to outwit and outmaneuver the parents, while the parents try to figure out how to keep control of the child.

It starts as soon as the baby leaves the womb. The baby is uncomfortable or hungry and begins to cry. We as parents go and pick the child up. We take care of that need and put the baby back down. The baby cries again because he or she may not want to be put down. You, the parent, pick the child up and the baby stops crying. Now the baby realizes how to get the parent's attention, and the games begin.

If the parent falls into that trap, he or she has a difficult time differentiating between the child crying for attention or the child needing to eat or having gone number one or two.

This is why we have to catch the children when they are

young—right out of the womb. Train that child and you will have a better chance of communicating with it as it grows. If the baby is crying and you know the baby is dry and fed, let the baby cry. The child will eventually realize that crying won't necessarily move you, and will only cry when there is the need. You win the first battle. It gets easier as long as you stay on top of things. That's not science, just my thought process.

There is often a disconnection between parent and child. If you lose connection with your child at an early age, trying to reconnect with them later in his or her growing process can be problematic. As parents, we often send our children mixed messages.

We try and establish rules and guidelines for our children. Now this is fine, if we can only stick to them. You as a parent can't just set rules and guidelines for your children and have the rules be flexible based on your mood or preoccupation.

If you punish your child for breaking a rule one day, he or she should be punished for breaking that rule every time. If you allow your child to break the rules based on how you are feeling, you are sending the child mixed messages and the games will continue. If it's wrong today it should be wrong tomorrow or any day after.

To the Child:

As a child, you know what is right and wrong, and even if you don't have the best parents in the world, you know they want only the best for you. Sometimes you have to help your parents help you.

You may not know this right now but your parents are your greatest allies. You know it because the first thing you do when you get into some trouble is scream for your parents. Do you remember when that big old dog chased you? The first thing you did was scream at the top of your lungs**, "MOMMMMMMMMA, DADDDDDY!"** If you have needs, go to your parents.

Don't rely on your friends for information that you should be talking to your parents about. That's like the blind leading the blind. If you take some dumb advice from a friend and get into trouble for it, you won't have to deal with your friends, you will have to deal with your parents. When you approach your friend about the dumb advice they gave you, they will stand there and give you the same stupid look you just gave your parents.

As a child you can't grow up by yourself; you need assistance. Who better to go to than your parents or the people who are responsible for you, who are obligated to you, and have an interest in you?

Don't isolate your parents. Keep them involved in the things that you are doing. It's about the team. You and your parents are a team. Communicate with your teammates, because when you win, it's a team win.

UNEDUCATED FOOL

This is such a crucial topic for both parent and child. We as adults should know that having an education is crucial toward becoming a responsible and productive adult. Somehow, somewhere, this may not have translated to the mind of the child, and that's because most of the parents still haven't figured it out themselves.

When I was growing up, the number one question about school was, "Why do I have to take the time to learn all of this stuff that I'm not going to use in my adult life? What does this stuff really have to do with what I'm going to be doing in life when I grow up?" **EVERYTHING!!!**

Here is the trick; this is where the teachers fall short. They spend more time teaching you the book stuff without putting you up on the game of life. It's like this: school prepares you for life as an adult. The things you are learning are not really the keys to productivity.

The keys are:

— Getting up out of bed on time to be at school on time.
— It's about getting to your classes on time.
— It's about having the right materials.
— It's about doing your work correctly and turning it in on time.

— It's about learning how to play and get along with others.
— It's about taking your homework home and doing it correctly and turning it in on time.

Those are the keys to becoming a successful and productive adult. If you don't do those same things as adults at your job—getting up out of bed on time, to be at work on time; getting to your job on time; having the right tools and materials; doing your work correctly and turning it in on time; knowing how to work and get along with others—you get fired!!!

It's about doing whatever it takes to keep yourself in good standing at work and in good graces with your boss. The better you do at your job the better chances you have at getting a pay raise or a promotion. The better you do in class the better your chances of improving your grades and the better chances you have of moving forward in life.

When I was elementary aged, I loved school. I loved learning and loved to read and write. When we moved from Indiana to California, what seemed to be a better life with more opportunities for my family turned out to be a downward spiral in my academic life.

The last time I graduated from school was in elementary. Elementary school was a controlled environment where we had one class and one teacher. When my father left, I was still in elementary. My grades were good but I wasn't getting anything else. When I began junior high school, that's when I absolutely lost my mind. Now that my father was gone, my mother had to work twice as hard, which meant I had more time to hang out with the neighborhood kids.

This is the time when everything went wrong for me. I began to hang out with the cats in the streets. I also began to smoke and drink. My grades began to suffer. Not only was I missing guidance, I was filling my brains with cigarettes, weed, and alcohol. I was getting street education from dudes who didn't know much about anything— including the streets. I had my mind on the wrong education.

In the eighth grade, I failed every class. I had over eighty-five absences and was able to keep it from my mother. I was eventually kicked out of the school district because of fighting. They still passed me to the next grade, though. I just believe they didn't want to take a chance of getting me back. My mother got fed up and eventually sent me to my father in Long Beach, California.

You would think this would be a great opportunity for me; I was getting a fresh start. My father was a human resource administrator for the Long Beach Unified School District. I went to Lakewood High School and was immediately put on the basketball team.

Here was the problem. I mentioned in the earlier part of this book that we are creatures of habit. I habitually didn't go to school in junior high, and I carried those traits with me to high school. I couldn't focus in class because I wasn't used to going to class. So, I eventually fell back into the same old ways: drinking, smoking, and not going to class.

This became a pattern and carried not only through my high school, but also through my limited college, right through my adult life. There is nothing worse than underachieving when you have all of the tools to become whatever you want to be.

As a child, underachieving was not a good thing for me, but I wasn't hurting anyone but myself. As an adult with children, I missed out on those days sitting with my sons going over their homework with them. I missed out on giving them the nurturing they needed. I realize that my absence affected their educational process, and they are still dealing with it right now, whether they know it or not.

As I spend time with my grandchildren, participating in their school events, I often think about the time I missed with my own kids. I know they think about it, as they see how attentive I am with their kids. No matter how successful I become I can never get back the time I should have spent educating my children. That's something I continue to live with.

To the Student:

It took me all of these years to figure this thing out, but I did. First of all, let's take this by steps. The first thing is that you have to go to school. There are no options. If you don't go to school they have created laws to take your parents to jail. So, it's understood that school is a must, whether you like it or not. So, if you have to go to school, then why not do the best you can while you are there?

That's what it takes to become a decent moneymaker. The better you are in school the greater your chances of earning great money. Without those things, you decrease your chances of being productive and happy, and increase your chances of drugs, crime, prison, and an early death.

The things you learn in school, as far as the technical things like math, English, etc., are all gravy. You may or may not use those things as an adult, but it doesn't really matter because you have to be there anyway, so why not learn.

The only thing worse than being bullied and teased in school is being ill prepared when it's time to take a test or participate in a class assignment. Do they still use the term rubbernecking? That's when you didn't take the time to study and you are trying to stretch your neck to look on the next person's paper because you haven't a clue as to what's on the paper in front of you.

Now this is difficult, because while you are rubbernecking, you are trying not to get caught rubbernecking. There is nothing more foolish than trying to look on someone else's paper to get the answers you should already know.

If you have the kind of teacher who watches the classroom closely, then all you can do is sit in your seat with that stupid look on your face, and that sick feeling in your gut, looking at a paper that's looking back at you. That is so embarrassing! But some of us, like me, did it time after time after time.

And how do you know if the person you are trying to cheat off of knows the answers? I guess you figure their answers have to be better than yours. Wow, that's so sad! But that's how I thought too.

The reason many of us fail in school is because we convince ourselves that we don't like school or that the work is too hard and we lose interest. If you tell yourself you don't like school, you won't like school. If you tell yourself it's too hard, the work will be too hard. That can also work in reverse. You have to go to school; don't be the only dummy not prepared.

For the children whose parents are just too busy, or for those who don't have that support from home, it's up to you to make it happen for yourselves. If there is something you don't understand, stay in your teachers face. Get with the kids who are smarter than you and ask them for help. Don't be embarrassed to ask for the help you need because it's not *how* you get what you need, it's *that* you get what you need.

If your parents or guardians aren't there for you, let that be the motivating factor that drives you to be the best you can be without them. I believe that you can do it. Give yourself a chance. As long as you care about you, and take care of your educational business, you are going to be all right. Don't let anything or anyone stop you from getting **YOUR EDUCATION!!!**

To the Parent:

I realize that you are busy but you should never be too busy to get involved with your kids education. I know this could be intimidating, especially when you look at what they are being taught and it looks like a foreign language.

Don't feel dumb because you may not understand what the kids are being taught. Don't use that as an excuse, because you would be letting down the child. It won't hurt you to sit with the child and find out what the child is doing. You would be surprised how much that would mean to your child.

Have you ever heard of "Two heads are better than one?" Of course you have. If the child is having trouble in school, the two of you can figure out what is the best course of action. There are tutoring programs in every school and there are also tutors off campus. Let's not forget the Internet search engines. They may not solve the problem but they could very well get you closer to understanding what the child is being taught.

So often, we get caught up with all of the things we have to do to keep the bills paid and the family running that we forget about our children. We hope they are doing what they are supposed to do. Let's not put that type of pressure on the children. Become a partner in your child's education. Yes, it will take some sacrifices, but trust me, it will be well worth it.

BULLY ME NOT!

This is a serious topic, and I want to make sure that I get this right. I want to make sure the kids getting bullied, the kids doing the bullying, and the parents of both sides understand the significance of this topic.

Kids can be some of the meanest and cruelest people on this planet. Some kids bully because they are hurting inside; something is missing in their lives but they can't relate to it. Often the problem comes from an unstable home environment where the child is abused in some way and takes it out on other kids to make them feel better.

Sometimes it comes from a stable home where the kids are provided with everything except for adequate communication between parent and child and the child lashes out because her or she feels entitled.

The kids who get bullied are often what other kids consider the nerds, the weak kids, the kids who are unpopular, the kids who don't have the latest in fashion, the fat kids, the kids with glasses and braces, or just the plain old smart kids. These kids are teased, picked on, beaten up, tricked, and talked about.

Now there is social media, and they have what they call cyber bullying! That is crazy! Now the kids get bullied all day at school, then they get bullied after school, and then they go home and get on their computer at night and get bullied all over again using social media!

I wasn't a bully when I was growing up, although I was bigger than almost all of my classmates. I was the one who took up for other kids who were bullied. I guess I did it because I had a kinship with the kids getting bullied. I was tall, really skinny, had nappy hair, and really big lips.

The one thing I had going for me was that I could fight and play sports, so I didn't get bullied to the degree of some, but they played mean tricks on me and they talked about me, so I understood what those kids were going through.

My father was a businessman, and really hip to his peers, but when it was time to buy me clothes he made sure that he bought me the cheapest clothes available. He would mix and match my clothes. He would take me to the grocery store and buy my shoes at the same place he would buy milk, bread, and meat. They were the cheapest shoes. They looked like Adidas but they had six stripes on each side. I tried to convince the other kids that my Adidas cost more because mine had more stripes. Crazy, right?

I didn't understand matching clothes at the time. He would buy me polka-dotted shirts and pants that had stripes. I don't know what my mother was thinking, allowing my father to dress me like that. I guess she felt he was a man and I was his son. Yeah, he was a man, but a man who needed a seeing-eye dog when it came to buying me clothes (I thought that was funny).

When you get older and have your own kids and responsibilities you no longer look at your parents in the same way. I called him cheap, but in actuality, he was just being practical. He could have been practical with a better color scheme. It would have made my life much easier, but oh well.

The funny thing is that I didn't think anything was wrong with the clothes and shoes until the other kids teased me. I was just happy to have new clothes, and shoes that I didn't have to put cardboard in the bottom to cover up the holes in them like I had to do in Indiana.

I tried not to let on that I was bothered by the constant teasing and being left behind when my neighborhood friends (who I thought were my friends), played together or went bike riding. It affected me deeply, much deeper than I ever realized. I was sad and I was lonely but pretended that I wasn't. I didn't want the other kids to know that I was hurting.

I've worn glasses practically all of my life. When it was time for me to get a pair of glasses, of course my father bought me the cheapest pair. I already looked like a goofball with the crazy-looking clothes and cheap shoes, nappy hair, big lips, and now I had to wear these crazy black glasses that took me over the top in goofiness.

When I was in grade school, there was this neighbor named Leonard. He was a real bully. He had these massive fists and he used to hit bricks with them. He tried to bully me, but I could fight and I would beat him up. He had a big brother who would then beat me up. This went on for some time. I didn't care about the beatings I took from his brother, because I would just turn around and do it to Leonard. I had to think his brother respected me for that.

When he realized that he couldn't intimidate me, not even with his brother, he used my need for being accepted to play cruel tricks on me. Once he broke into our house and stole our television sets. They were brand new; my sister and I had gotten them for Christmas. He would gather the other kids in the neighborhood and they would all play hide and seek; they were actually just hiding from me.

I had to fight almost every day until they realized that although I looked goofy, I was not the one to be messed with. I would have to fight the kids at my elementary school, and then I would have to fight their big brothers from junior high school.

One day I got so frustrated about being teased that I took my glasses off and I slammed them up against the handball court, shattering them into pieces. I didn't care about seeing or anything; I just wanted the teasing to stop.

I never told my parents what was going on with me, or what I had to deal with on a daily basis. I just took it as most kids do, not realizing that this kind of treatment could affect you for life.

I have to correct something. I said that I wasn't a bully, but when I got a little older and I was more accepted I would tease people who I thought were beneath me. I wouldn't physically hurt them, but now that I think about it, I probably hurt them as much as if I had punched them in the face. No one ever physically hurt me, either, but the things they used to say about me cut like a knife.

I totally forgot how it felt to be talked about and belittled. All I knew was cracking jokes on other kids, in some sick and twisted way, made me feel better. I was no longer the kid who took up for the kids who got teased and humiliated. I turned into one of the kids who was doing the abusing.

I couldn't see the hurt in the eyes of the kids who only wanted to fit in and not be the butt of jokes. I was destroying self-esteem while trying to repair my own. It's funny—writing this book, when I got to the bully part, all I could remember was being a victim of bullying, but never being the bully. I guess because I didn't physically hit kids, I believed what I had done was not considered bullying.

When I think about the kind of bullying I was responsible for, it was worse than the bullies who maliciously picked on and physically abused kids, because every kid I picked on considered me a friend. So, for them, it was a sense of betrayal. They understood being bullied by the kids who were malicious with it; they knew who they were. I blindsided them. I had a way of making you feel accepted and then I would take it away with a cruel joke. Not cool.

To the Bullied:

The best way to deal with a bully, and the most important thing, is that you must have confidence in yourself. I know that's hard when you're being called names like big lips, four eyed, fatty, skinny, goofy, nerd, ugly, and any of the mean names bullies use. The way you are now is not going to be the same as when you get older. I'm sure this doesn't give you much comfort now because you are getting bullied today.

If you believe in your heart that your life is going to be better as you get older then you are half way there. You are in control of how you are going to turn out in life; the bully is not.

If you look at the history of the kids who were bullied in school, many of those same kids have gone on to become some of the most successful and powerful people on this planet. You are the people who control how America is run because you are the people who had to endure the most.

Right now, you look at the bully as someone who is better than you—or at least more popular. You think that the bully's life is so much better than yours, but you don't understand the bully has issues too.

That is why they take their frustrations and problems out on you. As I spent time going in and out of jails and prisons, I saw the same kind of bullies you are dealing with right now. I was there with them all, because that is where most bullies end up.

The best way to deal with being bullied is to learn to laugh at yourself. The bullies get their power from making those who they deem defenseless miserable. The more you let the bully control your feelings, the better it makes them feel, the more power they believe they have over you, and the more they pick on you.

When the bully cracks a joke on you, laugh just as hard as everyone else. If you can, crack a better joke about yourself and laugh just as hard. This is not the easiest thing to do, especially when you are the butt of the jokes. Trust me, this will defuse the bully, because if you are not miserable, teasing you doesn't do anything for them. Also, the other kids will think you are cool.

This way is better than standing up to the bully by fighting them. It may make the bully stop bullying you, but you could very well get hurt or get into trouble. You can't fight everyone who has something negative to say about you, but learning to laugh at yourself makes it easier to deal with any other problems you may have.

This also can help you socially. It will open you up to communicate with others. Where you used to be shy and introverted, now you are able to communicate with others in a healthy way.

Don't take to heart what the bully has to say about you. Just because they say it doesn't make them right. You know yourself better than they know you, so it's ridiculous to take what they say seriously.

Trust me, this way of dealing with the bully will be a little difficult at first, but as time goes on it will get easier and easier until it just becomes second nature. When the bully realizes that they can't hurt you, they will stop. This also works with cyber bullying. You can defeat the bully just by believing in yourself, being clever, and outsmarting them.

To the Bully:

LEAVE KIDS ALONE! If you know what I know, you would treat those kids with the utmost respect. Those are the same kids who will grow up one day and will be the attorney who will represent you in a court of law, because the likelihood of you going to prison is great.

Look, bully, I realize you have issues and I'm not writing this book to point a finger at you or make you feel as bad as you make others feel. I'm writing this book because I know you can do better than what you are doing.

I believe in you, bully. I used to be just like you. Maybe you don't hear that often enough. Making other kids lives miserable—who may be having a difficult time already— to make you feel better about yourself is just not right. You can push a kid so far they snap and come back and kill you and a bunch of innocent kids. It happens much too often.

It's easy to pick on someone who can't defend themselves—coward, but easy. You know what is cool? What is cool is when you can go up to someone who you know is having a difficult time fitting in and sit down and eat lunch with him or her, or invite him or her to join in on some fun things that kids do. Say hello to that person, and give him or her a high five or a fist bump. No one is asking you to be BFFs, but a simple gesture would go a long way.

Do you know how that would make that kid feel? That's what should make you feel better! You have the power to change a kid's life with just a simple, kind gesture. You can do it, bully. I believe in you.

To the Parents:

Whether your child is the bully or the kid getting bullied, you need to know what is going on in your child's life. If your child is getting bullied, that child is suffering in ways that you can't imagine. If you pay close attention to your child there will be signs; you just have to look.

Communicating with your kids at an early age will make them comfortable enough to talk to you about the things that may be happening to them. Ask your kids questions. Look at your children closely. I know you love your kids, but can you look at them and tell that they may be having a difficult time with other kids?

If you see your child not having many friends, or your child seems isolated from other kids, that's a sign they might be getting bullied.

If your child's grades begin to suffer, that is another sign your child could be getting bullied. If your child begins to act out, that's another sign your child may be getting bullied.

For the parents who have children who are bullies, in many cases this has been brought to your attention before, but you can't believe your child would do such a thing. You discount what is going on because you feel you know your child so well; they couldn't possibly bully other kids.

You have to take the time to find out if your child is bullying other children and not believe some story your child comes up with. I realize that it is easier to just believe your child because it takes time to investigate— time you may not feel you have.

If you allow your child to bully other kids without taking the time to step in, you are just as responsible for that child's behavior as the child. Don't be blinded by ignorance. Take the time to find out what's going on with your child. You just may catch a problem before it gets totally out of control.

Parents, go through your kid's backpacks and computers. Watch and monitor their behavior. It just could be that your child is crying out for help.

SPORTS AND ACADEMICS

Sports play a very important role in many children's lives. They often watch their favorite professional teams and players on television, thinking of the day when they have a chance to get out there and become rich and famous.

Children join park leagues at a very young age for the fun of the game. Parents quite often get so caught up in game that they themselves lose sight of what's most important: the fun of the game. Some parents live their sports lives through their children, while others aren't there at all.

At a very young age, in the streets of Gary, Indiana, I often played different types of sports games. We lived in a poor neighborhood and usually we would play stickball because we didn't have bats. We would find any kind of ball and attach a bicycle rim to a tree and play basketball. We had big fun. I didn't know anything about organized sports but I was a true athlete.

When my father moved us out to California it was like night and day. Kids actually played with real baseballs and bats, and footballs and basketballs. There were even park leagues. This was different than the projects of Gary, Indiana, where all we had was what we created in the streets.

My father took me to join a park football league. It was amazing! We actually got real football uniforms. When I first received my football uniform and pads I walked around the neighborhood fully dressed. I'm sure the neighborhood kids thought I was mentally challenged. I was just so proud to be walking around in full gear, helmet included, for the neighborhood to see.

I only played one season of football because I really didn't like all of the contact. I was really skinny and it wasn't fun getting hit.

The next season I played basketball. The first time I hit the court I knew that basketball was my sport. I could play most sports well, but sports involving water over my head, like water polo or swimming, I was horrible at because I couldn't swim—still can't to this day. I swim like an anchor.

I played in park leagues, but I think after my father and mother split I never played anymore. I was a natural athlete and didn't have to do much as far as training. My mother was so into providing she really didn't have time for my extracurricular activities. My mother's boyfriend was not a sports cat, so I became a young gangbanger. Well, that wasn't the reason I gangbanged; I had choices but chose that life style.

When we moved to Inglewood, California, I played my ninth grade year. I really wasn't as good as I thought I was and I had an attitude. I was a freshman, and I played freshman basketball. I was embarrassed because I felt I should have at least played sophomore basketball.

I moved to Long Beach to live with my father and quickly gained a reputation as a standout basketball player at the nearby gym. That's where you pretty much got evaluated by the neighborhood. I figured I would play for powerhouse Long Beach Poly and so did everyone else. I lived right around the corner from Poly so I figured it was a no brainer. My father had a good friend who was the principal at Lakewood High School, so that's where I went.

I made an immediate impact as an athlete but my focus on my

studies was not there. Earlier in this book I said that we, by nature, are creatures of habit. I developed a disinterest in school in my junior high school years and it carried right with me into high school.

As a basketball player, I was a natural. As a junior I played varsity and led the league in scoring, which was a big thing because Long Beach Poly was the number two team in the nation.

As my name and face began to make the newspapers and colleges began showing interest, I became arrogant and I talked a lot of trash. The first letter I ever received was from Notre Dame. I really didn't even know the significance of receiving a letter from such a prestigious school like Notre Dame. I didn't realize the significance of getting a recruiting letter from any school.

I was one of those kinds of kids who you either really liked or your really hated; there was no middle ground. I was a ball hog. I wanted the ball and when I had it I was ready to shoot. In the middle of my junior year I had a season-ending leg injury.

I took it hard. It was difficult to sit out and watch my team play without me. Actually, they played better without me. They shared the ball and it seemed they were having more fun without me. What I should have done was sat on the bench and cheered for my teammates. I was too busy feeling sorry for myself.

The next season I was a senior and I had a better understanding of the game but the same twisted understanding about life. I was still missing school and they were just giving me grades to keep me alive to play basketball.

I believe my father was tired of me. He knew the road I was taking wasn't going to get me a scholarship or anything else. He would often tell me that I was in for a rude awakening, and he was right.

In my senior year my game was more rounded. I helped to motivate my teammates to shoot and got them more involved in the game.

For the first time in over ten years Lakewood High School made it to the CIF Tournament. We lost in the first round but it was still an achievement.

The season was over and I didn't even have enough credits to graduate. How embarrassing is that? I prided myself on being such a great student athlete, but I totally missed the student part. I was so embarrassed, not being able to walk across the stage to get my diploma. That was never a mission of mine. Crazzzzzy!

I went on to Cerritos College and tried it all over again. Once again, I had a really difficult time academically. I was growing as a basketball player, but as a man I was falling way short. There was emptiness in me that I couldn't shake.

One day I did something silly and got into it with Lorenzo Romar, the now coach of the Washington Huskies basketball program. He hit me with a basketball and I got so mad it was all I could do not to attack him, but I knew that would have been a bad move.

I decided to skip a year to get my head together. I was beginning to feel like the same thing that happened to me in high school was going to happen to me in college. When I came back the following year the head coach had taken ill and the assistant had taken over. He felt I had betrayed the team and the coach but he allowed me back on the team.

It was an amazing team without me, but with me, we were over-the-top amazing. My game had gotten better and I was going to classes. I don't believe the coach was going to allow me to stay. He played a bunch of games with me and was very nasty toward me. I made a mistake in a game and that's all he needed and he cut me.

Cerritos went on to win the state championship and I went on to a life of self-destruction.

To the Kids:

Playing sports is a wonderful thing to be a part of, but don't you think for one minute you can do it without getting your education. You can get an education without playing ball, but you can't play ball without getting good grades.

If you are good enough, sports should just be a way to get a free education. I missed that memo. I thought I was good enough to play major college ball and then go pro. I don't know how in the heck I thought I was going to play major basketball without getting my grades. I don't know what I was thinking! I guess I really wasn't. I wanted all of the benefits and rewards but I didn't want to work for any of it.

To top it all off, despite all of the college scholarship offers I received, I wasn't as good as I thought I was or I could have been, because it all came easy for me I felt I didn't have to work hard. I still chased the girls and smoked my weed and drank.

Listen, young men and women. A sport is an extracurricular activity that you can only participate in if you have the grades for it. If you are good enough, the school administration may assist you in getting the passing grades you need to stay on the team, but they won't be the grades for the classes you need to get into college.

When my days were done at Lakewood High School I didn't even have enough credits to graduate. They allowed me to continue to play because I was the star of the team. I was the only dummy who didn't recognize I was being used. When the last whistle blew I was treated just like any other failing student. I didn't graduate from high school or junior college. What a waste.

Utilize sports for what it is. If you are good enough, utilize it to get a free education. If I had been a true student athlete I would have gone on to play major college basketball and then gone on to the pros. The worst thing is I cheated myself out of a free education.

To the Parents:

It's really important to support your kids when they are playing sports. There is nothing more important in a child's development when they are playing sports than to look up in the stands and see their parents or loved ones cheering them on.

Some of you parents get overzealous and the game is more about you than about the child. Don't get so caught up that you take the fun out of the game for your child. Allow your child to experience the innocence of the game and to develop into the player they are going to become.

I wasn't there for my boys and I regret it to this day. Those are times that you can't get back. There is a hollow feeling every time I think about the time I could have spent with my boys, teaching them different sports. I cheated my children and I will regret that for the rest of my life.

TO BANG OR NOT TO BANG

MODERN DAY GANGSTA
Walking with pride, and a gun at his side,
from a young boy a gangster was born.
Leaving behind the ways of mankind,
and a family that one-day will mourn.
Trading books for a gun,
this boy on the run,
with a violent gaze in his eye.
Testing his skill,
this gangster will kill,
or at least till it's his turn to die.
Egos well blown, with a conscience unknown,
ruthless through intimidation.
Ruling the streets, not knowing defeat,
to his set is his only dedication.
Writing on walls, real big and small,
expresses his real claim to fame.
With cars that are dragging,

and pants that are sagging,
with a heart that is true to the game.
Ready to brag on his colored rag,
and the dangers that he has yet met.
Jumping into cars, going near or far,
shooting anyone not down with his set.
Yet keeping with times, and organized crime,
this popular gangster has spread.
Using cocaine as bait,
hopping from state to state,
to unfamiliar territories he treads.
With weapons advanced, the fear has enhanced,
this gangster is world widely known.
Never in life, has a gang caused such strife,
since the late days of Al Capone.
Big money's flowing, their numbers are growing, bigger and bigger each day.
Standing with pride, and a gun at his side,
ready to fight for his right to stay.
Blind with ambition, making real quick decisions, his path usually ends him in jail.
With prejudiced judges, and DAs with grudges,
to the sky goes this gangster's bail.
But never in doubt, and don't count him out,
soon he'll be back on the scene.
With pants that will sag, and cars that will drag, while copping a gangster lean.
Protecting his hood, for bad or for good,
violently his set he'll defend.
Testing his skill, this gangster will kill,
or at least till he plots his revenge.
So the police will sweep, some they will keep,

to a policeman a gangster scorned.
Whatever they do, one thing holds true:
every day a gangster is born.

I wrote that poem sitting in the Los Angeles county jail. I watched the gangbangers and wannabe gangbangers preying on people who they felt were weaker than them. I reflected back on my short stint as a gangbanger, reflecting on why I was attracted to that lifestyle and what it meant to me. Then, I began to write.

I realize that in a way the poem glorifies gangbanging, but then it's an actual account of the life of a gang member. Many gangsters who heard or read the poem identified with it. They felt a sense of pride, even though in the poem it said that they would eventually go to jail or die—like their life meant no more to them than to prepare for prison and death.

Of course none of them want to go to jail or die. They attend trials and funerals and they are sick of seeing their loved ones in caskets, or being led away in cuffs, but they go right back out into the streets with same mindset.

This is a really delicate subject because it's difficult to define what a gang is. To many, a gang is a group of young men and women, and oftentimes kids, who go around committing crimes and killing each other as well as innocent people. But to others, these gangs are friends and family to the people in their neighborhoods.

Whether you are born in a particular neighborhood or your parents relocate and you grow up in that neighborhood, you identify with other kids who are in that neighborhood, and the likelihood of gangs being in that area are great. These gang members are our sons, daughters, cousins, uncles, aunts, nephews, nieces, mothers, fathers, and sometimes grandparents.

When I first moved to California, it was in a really nice middle-class

Carson neighborhood. You would have never believed that a gang existed. I was about ten years old and my mother wanted to dress me like she saw some of the other boys dressed.

Back then, gang members wore colored bandanas in their back pockets to establish their gang. Well, my mother thought this was a fashion statement; she bought me Levis and my own array of colored bandanas. I know—hilarious, right? When she realized what the bandanas meant she quickly threw them away and then, of course, let my father buy my clothes.

When I think about it, I joined a gang for acceptance. Nothing we did was positive; nothing we did was productive. We drank alcohol, we smoked weed, we broke into houses, and we fought other gangs. Nothing we did prepared us for becoming productive citizens.

It was easy that way. We didn't have to work for anything. All we wanted to do was what we wanted to do, no matter who it hurt or how much it hurt us in the long run.

I remember the power I felt when I walked around with my Levis or khakis pressed with hard starch. My biscuits were spit shined. Biscuits were shoes with dots separating the tip of the shoe from the rest of the shoe, and we would polish the tips of those shoes until you could see your reflection in them. It's a trip! If I had been as diligent in my studies as I had been in polishing my shoes I could have been president.

We wore blue bandanas hanging out of our back pockets because our neighborhood was a Crip hood and Crips wore blue. I didn't know why they wore blue and the other side wore red. I didn't know what the gang stood for or how they got started. I didn't know anything. All I knew was that it was what it was.

We wore derby hats and we lined them with colored matchsticks in a decorative way. We walked around with walking canes, carrying weapons—mostly knives, but there were some guns. It was the mid 70s and I had finally been accepted by my peers and it felt great.

We lived in a middle-class neighborhood where none of the kids wanted for much. I guess we just wanted to be like the other neighborhoods. There was nothing really organized about what we were doing. We would sometimes fight other neighborhood gangs. There was some killing, but not much.

We eventually moved from our house in Carson and moved to Inglewood. I was checked into Inglewood High School. I didn't really know anything about Inglewood and didn't try to find out.

The first day of school, everyone I approached I greeted with, "What's up, Cuz." No one said anything, but looked at me strangely. As the day went on, I just went harder and harder, feeling more gangster than I ever had. When lunch came I sat down to wait for it to be over.

At the end of the campus there was a big crowd forming; it looked like a fight was about to take place. Usually, I would want to see the fight up close, but I just figured I would sit where I was since it was the first day of school.

As time went on, the crowd seemed to be getting closer. I thought, "Cool, if they get closer I might just be able to see the fight from where I am sitting." As they got closer, I began to hear what they were saying: "What's up, Blood! Inglewood Family Blood!"

I didn't know anything about Inglewood Family, but I definitely knew what Blood meant. I was totally devastated and I knew I was in big trouble. I didn't know what to do. I was in enemy territory and I didn't even know it. A crowd of about one hundred was descending on me and I couldn't run—one, because there was nowhere to run, and two, because I was frozen right in my seat.

They surrounded me, but nobody made a move. They just kept shouting, "What's up, Blood! Inglewood Family Blood!" Then it all died down and one of them asked me where I was from. Before my brain could respond my mouth was running.

"I'm from Leadership Gangster Player Crip!" I shouted.

It was a little offset gang from Del Amo Crip in Carson. They all just looked at me in stunned disbelief. Now, on the outside, I must have looked fearless, but on the inside I was crying and screaming like a big sissy. "Mommy! Daddy! Pleeeeeaase don't let them kill me! Oh, God, I will go to church every Sunday. I'll even eat my spinach!" I was praying to God.

Before I knew it God must have answered my prayer because security came from everywhere and dispersed the crowd. I was devastated because I had been so close to getting killed. I was so scared that I really couldn't move. I promised myself that I would never go back to Inglewood High School again.

I ditched school for about a week. Every now and again I would sneak out during the day and go to the store for a beer. I knew my presence was big news in Inglewood and I was a hunted little boy.

One day, as I went to the store, I saw a guy having a fight with some other dudes. I went over and gave him a hand. The other guys ran off and the guy and I sat down for a minute.

Because what I had done at school was such big news, he figured out who I was and asked me curiously what had happened at school. I told him what happened and he laughed so hard he was crying. He figured that I must have been the baddest Crip to ever walk the earth or the dumbest. I assured him that I was definitely the dumbest.

He liked me and tried to get me to join the Inglewood Family. I told him I didn't change gangs like that, and as a gang member I obviously didn't know what the heck I was doing. I told him that I was through with gangbanging and I wanted to just play basketball somewhere.

He suggested that I go back to Inglewood High School. I told him he was crazy and that I wasn't going back to Inglewood. He looked at me sternly, in my face, and told me to go back to school and that nobody would bother me. I was always kind of bold so I went back to school and believe it or not, nobody bothered me for as long as I was there. Nobody "Blooded me," and of course I didn't utter the word "Cuz" either.

It just so happened that the guy I helped out was one of the shot callers for the Inglewood Family and he gave me a pass. I never gang-banged again.

I wish I could tell you that I went on to live happily ever after, but that didn't happen. As far as gangs were concerned, they didn't affect me much, except for the many funerals that I attended. You have young men and women out there waging war against each other, killing each other for no other reason than because they feel that is what they are supposed to do.

In the early 80s the game changed. The Contra War was in full swing, and the United States was right in the middle.

From what I understand, the CIA came up with a brilliant idea that they could help fund that war by dealing with unsavory—and let's just say criminal—elements who were involved with drug trafficking into the United States.

I read a legal document that was so chilling to me I could hardly believe what I was reading. It was about a pilot who flew the drugs into the United States and the conspiracy that surrounded it. I will just leave it at that because this is not a political forum.

That is how cocaine went from being a drug that very few people could afford to a drug that everyone could afford. That was the crack boom of the 1980s. I'm not sure what affect the money had on the Contra War, but I sure know it escalated the gang war on our home turf.

What we do know is that cocaine was brought into the United States by the tons and was cut (mixed) with some kind of ingredient that heightened the level of addiction. It was then reduced into a rock form and sent right out into the ghettos of America.

The gangs saw what the drug was doing to the people in their communities and swore off using the drug, then they linked into big-time cocaine suppliers. Now the gangs had more money than they could ever have imagined, and with the money came the guns, and with the guns came death.

The gang war became real and turf had more of an importance than the color of the bandana. It wasn't just about having a place to patrol anymore; now it was about money. Territory meant money—the more territory you controlled the more money you made.

The death toll rose around the United States and the gangs were mobilizing. The government began to wage a war against some of its citizens by creating laws that focused on the lower-level crack dealers who were mostly minorities in poor neighborhoods.

Now the jail and prison business was booming and they were elated. The funeral business was booming. The crack cocaine business was equally booming.

The gangs were strong, powerful, and had plenty of money, and the government was making a great deal of money as well. It seemed for a while that the government and the gangs were in a partnership, with the gangs always coming out on the losing end.

I wasn't a gangbanger kind of cat, but I found myself wanting to belong. I had no one to tell me not to. This goes back to the parents. My mother really didn't' know anything about California gangs back then, but she did know a great deal about hard work. Many parents were so caught up in work they missed the signs.

This also goes to the father in a child's life. When my mother and father separated for good, I was missing a father for a time. Actually, my father and I were not that close anyway. I don't know why there was a disconnection between us. I think if we had it to do all over again, my father and I would have a different kind of relationship.

My father didn't know what I was going through as a kid. I'm sure I wouldn't have chosen gang life if my father and I had had a better relationship. He has learned over the years, by the way he raised my stepbrother, and by how he treats his grandchildren. That's why I say it's important for both parent and child to communicate with each other, no matter how awkward it may feel.

Most kids gangbang because the gang gives them the love they feel they don't get at home. Of course it's a misplaced love, but it's an in-your-face, hands-on kind of love. Sometimes a gang can make you feel invincible, even though you know your days could be numbered at any time. Being in a gang comes with a level of respect; it's something to belong to, but it also comes with a hefty price.

It's so difficult to see your child as a gang member, because in most cases they weren't raised that way. So when you see the parents on the news when their child gets killed, the first thing they usually say is, "My child didn't belong to a gang. He wasn't raised like that." If your child wasn't raised like that, what happened? Something happened! We just have to find out what.

To the Gangster or Wannabe Gangster:

The government is waging a war against you, and the police view you as public enemy number one. The government is creating laws that will put you away for the rest of your life, away from your family and friends, and away from living any kind of productive life.

It's crazy, because you are waging a war against each other, killing each other, and the system is trying to kill you. How can you win? You can't!

You are some of the most creative, strong, and brilliant people, but you are blinded by ignorance. You are assisting the powers that be to destroy you! That's crazy! I get it; it's about the hood. Everywhere you go there is a hood being represented, but it's not just that you represent a hood—it's how you represent that hood.

You are our children and we love you, but we can't stand by and allow you to destroy yourselves along with the lives of our children and our culture.

We realize that a lack of jobs makes it difficult to survive and lead a productive life, but don't let that be the reason you do the things you do criminally. You have to put yourself in position to win. Get educated; become an entrepreneur running your own business. Utilize that brain to do more than creating problems for yourself, your family, and the community you live in.

If you can run a lucrative criminal enterprise, you can run a lucrative legitimate enterprise.

To the OG (Original Gangsta):

As an OG and leader of your neighborhood you have a responsibility to assist with guiding our youth so that they may become productive citizens as well as world leaders. You can do it because I've seen you do it. I've seen you protect and give a pass to school-age athletes who have the potential of possibly becoming professional athletes.

You can do the same thing for the rest of the children in your neighborhood. Doesn't the average kid have the right to be backed by his or her OG home boys or home girls if he or she wants to become a doctor, lawyer, engineer, policeman, fireman, nurse, or whatever he or she wants to be other than an athlete? Shouldn't you look at that kid who is going to school and encourage him or her to keep on doing what they are doing?

How do you think kids would feel getting encouragement from an OG, whom they respect, to go to school and get an education? Encourage that kid to go to school. Cheer for that kid to be the best person they can be. Keep all of the negativity from that child and protect that child. Keep them from the same traps and from going down the same path as you. Now that's gangsta!

To the Parents:

There is no concrete way of keeping your kids away from gangs. Every time your child leaves the house there is a high probability your child will run into a gang member. What happens when your child runs into that gang member, to a degree, depends on you.

Kids gravitate toward gangs because they are not getting the necessary nurturing at home. I'm almost certain that if I had spent more time with my father instead of the kids in the streets then the gangs would have never got me. I left gang life when I was in the ninth grade. I joined the gang when I was in the seventh grade.

It all goes back to training your children early. In most cases kids are not pressured into joining the gang; it's generally a decision they make on their own. This is an ongoing theme of this book **STAY IN YOUR KID'S BUSINESS!** Look for signs early in your children's development. Never believe you know your kids enough that you don't have to check on them.

Look for signs of drug use, search for graffiti on notebooks, monitor their social media, etc. Monitor how they dress and whom they hang out with. Most of all, give them love, time, and your many years of wisdom.

For those parents who know they have gangbanger kids, I feel for you. We all know this is a tough position to be in, waiting for a call you know is inevitable. Stay on your children to make the correct decisions. Try using different ways to communicate with them. Don't give up on them. Stay in prayer and hope for the best.

DRUGGED OUT

I know drinking, smoking, and doing drugs seem like the cool thing to do as a young teen, but it's not even cool for adults. You sit back and see adults indulging, and I know it seems like they are having a bunch of fun. Trust me on this—there are two sides to this story.

The first side to the story is the part where it appears fun. In the moment, it always feels good. The substance makes you feel different, altering your natural state of mind. It may even make you forget about your problems. Things seem funnier. You may feel happier. Sometimes, it may make you feel cooler or part of the crowd. It may make you feel like you are more of an adult. This side is short lived and deceptive, lasting only hours at best.

Then there is the consequential side, the side that lasts a lot longer. This side will have you sick to your stomach, vomiting until you feel your guts turning inside out. This is the side that will have you hooked, selling your body, and stealing from friends and family.

This is the side that will have you spending countless years in prison. This is the side where you watch the US Marshalls come and put you out of your house in the early morning hours because your parents, one or both, messed off the money on that substance.

This is the side where you flunk out of school. This is the side where you are taken away from your parents. This is the side where you are out and someone slips something in your drink and takes you away and rapes you. This is the side where you could die well before your time. This is the side that has long and lasting affects.

I was about six when I had my first taste of beer. My parents were social drinkers and liked throwing parties. Adults often let the kids sip a little beer, thinking it was cute when they get a little tipsy. I didn't like the taste, of course, but I thought it was cool to be around adults doing what adults did.

My mother and father never encouraged me in that way, but I was privy to what they were doing. They never thought, as most parents don't, that what they were doing would have any influence on their children.

My mother was a cigarette smoker and at the age of twelve I experimented with the rest of the neighborhood kids. I really didn't like smoking, either, but I felt cool doing it. I remember, once, my mother found a cigarette on me and she told me that if I was going to smoke she would rather me smoke at home. When she told me that I was like, "Man, I'm almost grown!"

I should have known it was a trick because I went out and got one of the big homies to get me a pack of cigarettes, and when I brought them into the house and tried to light one of them up she took them away from me and smoked them herself. I wonder, if I had bought a different kind of cigarette other than the kind she smoked, would she have let me keep them. Nah!

Around the same time, I graduated to weed. I stopped smoking cigarettes but kept drinking and smoking weed. That was around the same time I joined a gang.

The substance abuse and gangbanging seemed to go hand in hand, but what I found out later on in life is that substance abuse also went hand in hand with college, sports, entertainment, and almost everything else. I'm getting a little ahead of myself.

My father and mother divorced and my mother married a man who smoked marijuana, so this became convenient for me. My mother didn't approve, so of course we kept it away from her. Drugs and alcohol are one of the reasons I did so miserably in school.

I know some of these occurrences are overlapping, but that's what happens when you use drugs throughout your life. They seem to intertwine with the sequences of events throughout your life.

I was the kind of kid who didn't mind trying new drugs. I was in junior high school and I had already tried cocaine, angel dust, and different kinds of hallucinogens. My mother didn't know because she was working hard every day and I was good at staying out of the way.

One night, in the summer before I was to enter the tenth grade, I was allowed to go to a house party with a few friends. We all decided to chip in and get some weed. When we got to the weed spot they didn't have any weed but they did have what they called a "sherm stick." I didn't know what a "sherm stick" was and by the look of it I immediately wanted a refund of my $1.50.

What I found out later was that a "sherm stick" was made from the same substance used to make angel dust. Instead of soaking the mint leaves in the solution, (embalming fluid and a bunch of other brain-damaging mess), they dipped a Nat Sherman cigarette into the solution, thus the name sherm stick.

All of the other boys knew what it was and took small puffs, but when it got to me, I tried to get my money's worth and I sucked it up like it was weed. All I can remember was that I saw this pretty young girl I wanted to dance with. I went over to the DJ and asked him to play a slow song. I sat down to wait for the song and I never got back up.

I sat there and couldn't move. I could see everything, and I could hear everything, but I couldn't move and I couldn't talk. I just sat there, as people came to look at me as if I were on some kind of display. I wanted to scream but I couldn't. I found out later that one of my friends was up on the roof and couldn't get down. My other friend was racing himself up and down the street. Yes, you read this right: the young man was racing himself up and down the street.

Back then they called it "water," or "butt naked" because it would make some people take their clothes off. They still use it today, but the potency is not the same. Back then some people lost their minds and never got them back. They walk the streets to this day like zombies. It is really a sad sight.

Believe it or not, I continued to smoke that stuff—but not that much, and I was at least smart enough to hit it once and put it down. One day I hit that stuff a few times and went home. My sister was cleaning up and she kept talking to me. It seemed like her voice was penetrating my brain and I couldn't get her to shut up. I picked up a knife and started chasing her with it.

Fortunately, that stuff had me going in slow motion and she got away. It could have been a real tragedy. That was the last time I used angel dust, sherm, or anything that had anything to do with embalming fluid

In high school, I still smoked my weed, drank a bit, and if I got ahold of some cocaine I would use it—but not much. Then the 80s came in. There was a big fight going on with Larry Holmes and Jerry Cooney, The Great White Hope. Larry beat the heck out of Jerry and an older friend of mine won a lot of money off of some fool who bet on Cooney.

He celebrated by buying a lot of cocaine and he did something I had never seen before, but I had heard Richard Pryor talk about it on his albums: freebase! My friend rocked that powder up some way and broke out these glass pipes. He tried to show me how to smoke it but I kept messing up and he told me to stop wasting his money.

At that time you had to have money to buy cocaine. Cocaine was a high for the rich, so you know it had to be a surprise when cocaine found it's way into the hood and was as available as buying a dime bag of weed. Before that there was no cocaine addiction in the hood—nobody could afford it, especially to freebase it.

I used to watch people getting hooked right and left. I just couldn't understand how they could get hooked. I had tried it and it didn't do anything to me. I had cousins who had gotten hooked and all I could do was shake my head. I looked at them as if they were weak because I knew it couldn't happen to me.

Cocaine was being bought and sold in rock form, and that's what they called it: "rock cocaine." It was pretty cheap, and I saw people making tons of money off of it and I wanted in. My basketball aspirations were all but over and I was always trying to take the easy road, so the first thing I did when I got a little money was buy some rock cocaine. They eventually called it "crack;" I guess that came from the East coast.

Remember, I was always one to try anything, and when I finished breaking up the rocks I was going to sell I had a little left over— what they called crumbs. I had my cousins with me, and of course they were going to help me sell, so we used their pipe to smoke the crumbs.

When I hit it, it didn't feel like it felt when I first tried it. This was a different kind of feeling. It went right to the part of my brain that occupied my pleasure nerve, or dopamine.

The next thing you know I was hooked! I became a crackhead, just like my cousins and everyone else out there that were crackheads. I stole from friends and family. I wrecked my marriage. I kept telling myself that I could sell it, that I was better than the rest of the people who were smoking it.

In my lying mind, I felt like I was the one who was making money. My wife at the time would work hard Monday through Friday, and because she loved me, and believed in me so much, she would give me money and I would go out there to buy more cocaine.

Each time I would start off great but I would always come back broke with no money and a sad story. The feeling that I was going through when I got down to the last little bit of crumbs was as horrible a feeling that a person could feel. I would dig holes in my pockets trying to find imaginary dope that I made myself believe was there.

I would be on my knees in search of crack on the floor. I would be physically sick and desperate when I knew I couldn't get any more. I smelled so bad, because I would have been up for days without bathing. I had lost so much weight it was scary. I didn't care what anyone thought of me because the only thing on my mind was smoking crack.

I went through this for several years, looking like the walking dead. I messed up some gang member's dope they fronted me because I told them I wanted to sell for them. They beat me within an inch of my life. The really crazy thing about the entire situation is that I was a bloody mess from head to toe and all I could think about was hitting the pipe. My crack friends just looked at me in disbelief. You know you are in bad shape when other crackheads are looking down on you.

I stole a friend's Christmas money she had for her kids. I was sick because she was a really good friend to me. Then a dude, probably on crack himself, tried to rob me at gunpoint of the money I had stolen from her. I was so strung out I wasn't about to let him steal the money I had stolen. I took the gun from him and chased him with it, and then sold it for crack. I hate what I did to my friend because she is an amazing person.

My stepfather, who I began smoking weed with at twelve, and my stepbrother also got hooked on crack. I was the worst, because I was in the streets living every day for the drug. I didn't want to have sex. I didn't want to eat. All I wanted to do was smoke crack.

Once I smoked up some money that I shouldn't have. I owed my then mother-n-law some money, my wife's car was out of gas, and

I was broke. I didn't know where I was going to get the money, so I robbed an establishment.

I had broken into houses before when I was a child but I had never walked into any place pretending to have a gun and rob it. I was able to pay my mother-in-law back, put gas in the car, and of course had enough to buy some crack. I never did that again, but I would eventually do other things.

This is how crazy it got. I was visiting this female at her family's place. I went to the back and left the door unlocked. I went back later looking for something of value to sell. My mind was so twisted that when it was time for me to choose between a brand new VCR or a long 22. rifle, I chose the rifle. You are probably wondering why I didn't choose them both. Well, I didn't have a car so I had to choose one or the other.

I wrapped the rifle in a sheet, thinking this would disguise what I was carrying. I walked down a major street, to catch a bus, looking like a tall black fool carrying a rifle wrapped in a sheet. I could have easily chosen the VCR and no one would have been the wiser.

Well, I quickly caught the attention of bystanders who quickly called the police. I don't know what I was thinking. I had to look like a crazy man, walking down the street with what looked like a rifle in a sheet.

The police pulled up in force. They didn't approach me immediately but followed me for a few blocks. I could only guess they were trying to find out what in the hell I was doing. They probably couldn't believe what they were seeing.

I think they called backup just to verify what they were seeing. I was walking down the street as comfortably as if I were carrying a loaf of bread. That's what that dope will do to you. Of course they took me to jail.

I eventually cleaned up and stopped smoking crack. I had even gotten a job as a customer service rep at the Marriott Hotel. This wasn't a bad job for a dude with no education. I had to get up at about 3 a.m. just to make it to catch three buses to get to work. It took me three hours to get there and three hours to get back, and I had to work eight hours in between.

On my way from my apartment, walking to the first bus stop, I would pass this motel. It was no more than a dope spot and it had nonstop activity. This is how drugs work. All I could do was think of how much money I had lost doing crack, and how crack had beaten me. I was tired of catching the bus and I wanted a chance to redeem myself. So I quit my job and took my last paycheck and bought an ounce of cocaine.

This all goes back to decision-making. I could have taken that money and bought a car so I could continue going to work at a major hotel. I could have worked my way up and established myself in that company, collected benefits, taken care of my children, and eventually retired.

That was too much like right. I was caught up in my own self-worth, believing that cocaine had defeated me. I was treating crack like it was a human with feelings and emotions; it had defeated me and I wasn't going to let it get away with it. I was going to defeat crack, if it was the last thing I ever did. That is hilarious, I know.

I bought an ounce of crack with my last paycheck. That night, I put it on the shelf and tried to go to sleep. Every time I closed my eyes they would pop back open. I began to have the farts. My stomach was bubbling. You see, that is what addiction does to you; it not only affects your mind but it also affects your body.

I never smoked crack again and I became a pretty successful crack dealer. I took over the little motel spot and I was raking in thousands a day. You would think that would be the end of my problems, but they were just beginning.

The local police knew who I was but I didn't care. I felt like I was smarter than they were. One morning, I decided to take my girlfriend to breakfast at the local breakfast spot. When I walked in, it seamed like the entire police force was in there. I smiled and nodded my head and casually sat down to order. They sat there for a few minutes and they all left at the same time.

I went back to my spot at the motel to check my trap; one of my runners told me the police had the entire motel surrounded. I wasn't concerned because I didn't have any drugs on me so I sat and played video games with a young kid.

One of my old-time friends came to the door and asked me if I had any dope. I asked if he saw that the place was surrounded. He was so strung out that he tried to convince me that the coast was clear.

I believed my runner because I had just left the police at the restaurant and I knew I was surrounded. So I told my old-time school buddy to take my car and make a right out of the motel. I lived to the left. As soon as he pulled out in my car and made that right turn, the police were on him. There had to be twenty cars after him. I casually walked out of the motel and made a left and walked home. They were upset and roughed him up a bit for being so stupid.

As hooked as I was on smoking crack, I was just as hooked on selling crack. The money was good to me and I liked it. I believed I had come back from hell and I deserved that money. I felt it was vindication. I didn't care about the lives I was ruining. I didn't care that I was once in the same situation these crackheads were in, and not once did I put myself in their position, because I had already been in their position.

I was fronting crack to people who were addicted to crack, and I would raise hell when they were short on my money; at times I would beat them like I had gotten beaten. Once I had snuck into the hotel at about 3 a.m. and began to beat the people who had messed up my money. I woke them up with a stick.

Who was I to beat anybody because they were addicted to crack and did what I had done when I was addicted to crack? I was a hypocrite to the highest degree. After that night I had to change my approach on selling crack. I stopped the violence but kept ruining lives.

Another friend of mine from college had gotten strung out and he messed up some of my money. I told him he had to get my money some kind of way. I took him to a check-cashing place and gave him an ax and told him to go and get my money. He just sat there and stared at that ax.

He didn't take the ax but came running back to my car with a wallet in his hand, screaming, "Chuck, I got it! I got it!" I pulled off and watched him in my rearview mirror, screaming my name and holding up the wallet. I couldn't even be mad at him, because that wasn't his life. I immediately took him to the Navy Recruiting Office and he became a Navy Seal.

I was about to drop off a fresh sack of crack at the motel spot, and I was walking up the stairs when a black and white pulled in. When they saw me I was stuck. I tried to run up the stairs with the sack in my hand. I didn't have a key and they were right on me. They got me with the dope and I went to jail.

I needed to go to jail, because I could have easily gotten killed. I was a drug dealer all by myself and could have been a victim of a robbery or someone could have just wanted my spot and killed me for it. I could have killed somebody, because the drug world is no place to play games. It is an all-or-nothing business, and if you are not with it, it will get you killed.

When I got down to the police department, it was like they had just caught Al Capone. They were popping champagne bottles and everything. I had never been to prison and ended up getting three years.

The crazy part about the whole thing is that when I got back out of prison I went right back to what I knew, and what I was successful at: selling drugs. At least that's what I told myself. Actually, as always,

I was taking the shortcut to making my money because I really didn't want to work hard for it. I didn't want to get educated to better my position. I just wanted to make money the easiest way possible.

I was also a part of this nonprofit organization that was supposed to help the inner city. The entire thing was a joke and I was a hypocrite. I would leave my dope spot and fly out to speak to businessmen about the problems in the inner city, and I was one of the problems.

It was January and we were invited to the White House for the National Prayer breakfast. I sat with several Congressmen and must have impressed them because when I got back to the hood my pager was going off. I left such an impression on them that they asked me to lead the prayer for reconciliation for the State's Prayer Breakfast at the state capital in California.

I hung up the phone and began walking down the street. I was very disappointed in myself because there I was at the White House in the presence of the president of the United States of America and I was no more than a no-good drug dealer. I immediately went to my spots and told my workers they could keep the money and the dope. I was done and never sold drugs again.

Although I was free from cocaine, I still smoked marijuana, and although I didn't view it as a problem, it was. Once, I was doing some white-collar fraud in Indiana, Kentucky, and Tennessee in a rental car and I was cruising on I-65 smoking on weed. Suddenly, this little sports car pulled up behind me and to my surprise turned on its police lights.

I was high and tripping because I had never seen an unmarked sports police car before, so I put the joint out and let down the windows to try and air out the car. I finally pulled the car over and the officer stepped out of the car.

My mind was racing; I was high as a kite and I knew I was going to jail. He asked me about the weed. I reached over and handed him the ounces I had in the bag. As he looked into the bag, for some reason I punched the accelerator and took off. The police officer jumped into his car and began to follow me.

Before I knew it, there had to be thirty cars giving chase. I don't know what I was thinking. I was high out of my mind and in the middle of nowhere. Big rig trucks were trying to run me off of the road. Then, a police car had gotten ahead of me and tried to lay down spike strips to bust my tires, but I swerved around them and kept going.

It began to rain a little and I had to make a decision. I decided to exit, trying to fool the police, but my tires locked and I flew over an embankment. I had to be thirty feet in the air. All I could think of was that I was going to die.

I was flying over a cornfield when the car finally landed on all four tires, deploying the airbag. I quickly checked myself and was amazed that I wasn't injured at all. The next thing I did was run; I got the fraudulent checks out of the trunk and began running through the cornfield, tearing them up. Yes, of course I went to jail. If I hadn't been smoking weed I would have never gotten caught, at least not at that time.

I wish I could tell you that I lived happily ever after, but as you know by now that's not what happened. As you read this book you will find that drugs played a big part in my life. I was already fighting an uphill battle with my decision-making and my lack of a solid foundation and the necessary tools to make it in the real world, not to mention my many character flaws.

When I was on crack, it was the worst time in my life. That drug controlled my every movement and I didn't know what to do to get out. When I sold drugs, the end result was just the same. I just had to do more time in prison for selling.

As a young child growing up you have no business messing with drugs of any kind. The short-term feeling of happiness doesn't add up to the long-term affects and life long suffering.

To the Parents:

Don't be afraid to go into your kids room and search. Never think you know everything about your children and never put anything past your children, because once you do, they will disappoint you.

Don't be afraid of talking to your children about drugs and alcohol. Don't get mad at them if they tell you something you may not approve of. It's better to know now than to find out later when you are getting that phone call that all parents dread.

Trust me, I know; drugs kept me away from my children. When I was using, I was too consumed by the drug. When I was selling, I was too consumed in selling the drug. Then there was the time I lost from my kids when I went to jail and prison because of the drugs.

If you are parents with young kids, that's the reason you train them early. Get to know your kids. Make them feel comfortable enough to communicate with you.

Watch what you do around your children, because trust me, they are watching every move you make. They are not going to do what you say; they are eventually going to do what you do.

To the Kids:

Don't be so quick to grow up. Drinking, smoking cigarettes, and doing drugs does not make you grown or closer to being an adult. All it will do is take you to a place you don't want to go.

I know, I know you, are going to do what you want to do anyway, but let me tell you: with that way of thinking you will be sitting in a jail cell thinking about how stupid you were and how it could have all been avoided.

When I was using drugs as a kid, all I was doing was stifling my potential. I was never my best at anything on any drug, weed included.

Drugs were a result of me not having an adequate education.

Drugs and alcohol are direct results of the many problems people have in their lives. Many use drugs to forget about their problems, but when that high comes down the problems are still there. Give yourself a chance to make it in life. At least, wait until you become an adult to make the decision to use or not use.

POOR CHOICES COULD MEAN JAIL/PRISON

If you are a normal person when making a stupid decision, there is a moment of indecision. This is the time that actually defines the direction you are headed in your life. If you are headed in a positive direction, the process will be simple. It usually begins when you are young.

If there is something you want in the store but you don't have money to pay for it, but you want it desperately, there may be a momentary thought in your mind to just steal it. You know it's wrong to steal, and if you get caught you could get into big trouble. So, you take a long, sad look at it and you walk out of the store without it.

Now, if you are headed in the wrong direction in life, and you see something in the store that you really want but you don't have any money to pay for it, there will be that same momentary thought in your mind. However, the desire for what you want will outweigh the consequences of getting caught and you will steal it.

Your lying mind will convince you that you won't get caught; if you don't get caught that time, your lying mind will convince you that you will never get caught, until you actually get caught. Then your lying mind will be exposed for the liar it is while you are sitting in a jail cell.

When I was a young kid I never got caught for any of the stupid and illegal things that I had done. It wasn't until I was around nineteen years old and in college when I got caught and did my first stint in jail.

I was in college and had a little apartment by the beach. I also lived near this motel that I used to cut through to get to my apartment. Although I was in college, I still had many of the same character flaws I had when I was gangbanging, such as smoking and selling weed. I was just a small-time hustler who always tried to take the easy way through life, even though I was a college athlete.

One day while going through the motel I found several keys to rooms. After collecting several more keys I began to rent the rooms that weren't occupied at the time, hourly, to people who needed a room for an hour or so. I took a girlfriend's brother with me to check on the rooms and he tried to break into an adjoining room and I got caught.

The police had us sitting on the curb. I tried to tell the police officer that we were just walking through the motel to my apartment, but when they checked him, he had motel soap, shampoo, and lotion. The cold part about it was he didn't even bathe regularly and he was stealing soap and shampoo!

I had heard a lot about jail from television and mostly from my big homies who had done time before. I thought I had to go in there hardcore to let people know I was ready for anything they came with. Actually, I was scared out of my wits and I didn't know what to do.

While riding to the police station in the back of a black and white police car, my hands were handcuffed behind my back so tightly that I thought my hands were going to fall off. Fortunately for me I was only minutes away from the police station, but because the cuffs were on so tight it seemed like hours.

When I walked into the station, I became super hard. I was acting like I had just killed ten people and robbed twelve banks. That was on the outside, but on the inside, I was crying for my mommy and daddy like a big baby. I realized very quickly that I really didn't have to act hard but I did have to mind my own business.

I didn't think what I had done was a big deal. I had never been in jail before and I was a college basketball player, so I figured I would be out in no time. They took me to the Long Beach Police Station. It was filled to capacity and it was cold and very uncomfortable. Because it was my first time, it seemed that everyone who had done any kind of time wanted to assist me with my case. These unique invaduals are called jailhouse lawers. They never went to law school but have been in jail so many times they feel they know everything about the judicial process.

The beds were hard medal with thin mattresses on them. The food was horrible and the place was dirty. There were all kinds of men in there for all kinds of alleged crimes. Everything that everyone was saying sounded like they knew exactly what they were talking about, but there were just so many angles and everyone sounded right. I was really confused, but most of them felt I was going home directly after court in a day or so.

Of course, all I wanted to hear were the scenarios that said I was going home right after I went to court. I was so attached to that scenario that I didn't even use the telephone to call anyone.

When I went to court I was all ready to tell the judge my side of the story so he would let me go, but that didn't happen. All I was allowed to do was to plead guilty or not guilty. I tried to talk to the judge but he wouldn't have any of it. All he said was, "Guilty or not guilty?" I said not guilty and was remanded back into jail until my next court date in two weeks, or at least until I bailed out.

My charge was commercial burglary. I didn't even know what

commercial burglary was. All I thought was, how could I burglarize a commercial? I was put back into the holding cell and that's where the nightmare really began.

Everyone who was unfortunate enough not to get out was headed to the LA County Jail. The LA County Jail is a great deal different now than it was back then.

We were all hooked up on four-man chains and were escorted onto old black and white buses. The ride to LA County would be the last bit of sunlight I would see until my next court date—or at least until I bailed out, which was unlikely.

I thought my stay in Long Beach City Jail was hell, but nothing could have prepared me for what I was about to encounter. Busses were brought in from all over Southern California. When they got everyone off of the busses we were jammed into various cells. It smelled so bad in those cells.

People came from all walks of life; there were killers, robbers, thieves, rapists, and many other types of deviants. But the sheriffs were just as bad as any of the prisoners, and some even worse.

We were moved around like cattle. We were talked to and treated like we were animals by the sheriffs. We were told to line the walls and empty our pockets. We were told to remove our clothes, and we were standing shoulder to shoulder. The stench was almost unbearable as we were instructed to bend over and spread our butt cheeks so the Sheriffs could see if we were smuggling anything up there.

They eventually shuffled us into the shower area, where we were sprayed with water and powdered with some kind of substance and handed what they called county blues (blue overalls). We were stuffed and packed into jail cells for hours on top of hours.

This is what they call, "in processing" or "classification." You would be housed based on your classification. If you were a known gang member, you would be housed in the gang module. If you had mental health issues, you would be housed in what the inmates called the "Ding Unit." If you were gay, they would put you in the "Gay Unit." If you were in on a major case or classified with extreme violence, they would put you in what they call "High Power."

Everyone else would be housed in other parts of the jail in general population. When you were just coming into the county jail and going to court, at that time you were most likely housed in the 9000 unit.

The most notorious dorm was 9500. This was a general population dorm, but it was crazy; robberies, rapes, and beatdowns were common in that dorm. The reputation of 9500 was wide spread. That dorm is one of the reasons for segregation in the LA County Jail today—that, and the war between the blacks and Hispanics of course.

When you were done with your sentencing and waiting to be transferred, they would put you in a small four-man cell that housed six inmates. The conditions were so horrible; the toilet was actually inside of the cell, and when your cellie had to use it, you had to sit or lay down there while he was taking a dump. Crazy!

I was in 9500 and I was terrified. I didn't hang with anybody, or claim any hood, so I was on my own. The living conditions were horrible and I just couldn't sit down and use the toilet. As a matter of fact, I refused to sit down on those deplorable toilets, and besides, after my court day I figured I was outta there anyway.

The sheriffs seemed to be constantly on me. I figured because I was tall they may have targeted me. I was trying to figure a clever way of making it light on myself, so as I was walking down the hall coming from chow (cafeteria) I just fell out on the floor and acted like I had passed out. They took me to the infirmary and I thought I was safe.

When I got down there, inmates were bandaged up, beat up, and torn up by police dogs. I don't know what I was thinking. It looked like I had jumped from the frying pan right into the fire. I thought I saw a man blink, "Please help," with his eyes. All I was thinking was I had to get out of there and back into 9500; it looked like people were dying in the infirmary. It looked like a war zone.

So, I got back up at 9500, and I waited for my court date. I still hadn't sat down to use the toilet, because I refused to sit in such stank conditions. I was a college basketball player and I told them that I wasn't going to be in there that long anyway.

It was two weeks later. I was back from court and back at the county jail, and I still hadn't sat down and used the toilet. So, finally, realizing that I wasn't getting out anytime soon, I finally relented and sat down on the toilet. Unfortunately, I waited too long and it came halfway out and got stuck. They had to call the jail doctor to assist me.

I know that's funny, but it wasn't funny then. I was stuck on the toilet when the sheriffs came to count. My bunk was empty and they thought I had escaped. An inmate pointed to the toilet area and that's where they found me. That was so embarrassing. They almost beat me up until they realized my problem.

I finally went back to court and they gave me probation. I had been in jail for a little over a month. In the early part of this book, I mentioned that I stole a rifle and went to jail. That time they gave me ninety days and a joint suspension of three years. That's just a trap. They put that joint suspension on you because they know that once you violate your probation they have the option of sending you away for those years suspended over your head.

When I got busted for possession and distribution of crack cocaine, my county jail time was a bit different. My bail was over $100,000 and I couldn't bail out, so I was in jail for as long as the case went.

This time I was going to prison. I guess, given the way I lived my life and the decisions that I was making, prison was inevitable. The LA County Jail was still rough and I knew I had a long time before I could even get my time. Just as I got into my dorm, I was really tired, but I wanted to use the phone to let my people know where I was and that I was okay.

As I waited for a free phone I saw dudes peeping me out but I didn't know why. I saw them forming and it looked like they were forming against me. They were banging on me as if I were the enemy.

Now you must understand that the general population— especially if you were black—was run by Crips. So if you were a Blood, or thought to be a Blood, you would be in big trouble. What it seemed happened was this little dude wanted my brand new shoes, my Gazelle glasses, and a diamond ring I had on my finger, so he tried to put a Blood jacket on me—which means he accused me of being a Blood gang member.

The way the dorm was made, the police were behind glass, elevated above us all in an angular position as to gain a better view of the entire dorm. These dudes are hopping over bunks, screaming "Cuz," and shouting out their hoods. I lived in Long Beach but I didn't claim a hood because once I stopped gangbanging, I stopped gangbanging!

I guess these guys figured I was a mark. Although I was really skinny, I was still 6'6" and I don't think they wanted to try and really see what I was about one-on-one.

I knew I had to think quickly, so I turned toward the window where the sheriffs were and knocked to get their attention. The Crips or wannabe Crips started turning away, screaming, "Ahhhhh man, look at this dude." But they all backed away and went in another direction.

The sheriff asked me what I wanted and I said that I didn't want anything. These fools really thought I was supposed to get beat down because of some code. I abided by all of the jailhouse codes, but I wasn't going to let a bunch of suckers beat and rob me. That wasn't happening.

A few of them walked up to me and asked what I was in for. I told them that I was in for possession and distribution of crack cocaine.

They asked me if was I going to prison. I told them that I was surely going to prison. They went on to say that I wouldn't make it because I had broken the code, but before he could finish I broke something down to him.

I asked him what set he was from, and if he was getting any time. Then I told him that people like me run the prison. I was going to be a clerk and I told him that when he gets where he's going, he better pray that the hood he's claiming is claiming him.

In prison, you have cats trying to claim hoods so that they can get protection. That works somewhat at the jail level, but it doesn't fly at the prison level. They will check your credibility in prison, and if you are not where you say you are from you will have big problems.

I went to court the next day, and when I got back to the jail I went back to the same dorm, on the same bunk that I had left. When those other cats came back and saw me in the same spot they knew I wasn't scared and treated me with respect, because they knew I could have gotten out of that dorm and into another one without a problem.

Things didn't go much better for me; because of my charges I was put into maximum security. Maximum security is where some of the roughest of the rough are housed. I don't know why I was put in there but by this time I just went where they put me.

Somebody had stolen some of my things, and I went up to the shot caller, (the gang leader) in the fifty-man dorm and I expressed some things to him. I explained to him that before I became a successful drug dealer I was a crackhead. I showed him my paperwork; on it was what my charges were and what I had when I was taken into custody. I wanted him to know what was stolen from me was nothing, but the only thing I had left of any kind of value was my glasses.

I explained to him that when I was a crackhead, I didn't care if I could see or not. I expressed to him that the glasses had no real monetary value other than the fact that I needed them to see and I didn't want them messed with.

He liked the way I came at him and assured me that he would do what he could to make that happen. When I went to sleep that night I placed my glasses under my mattress; when I woke up they were gone.

A sick feeling came over me, but at the same time I was pissed off.

"I told y'all not to mess with my glasses but you are going to try me anyway!" I shouted.

I didn't know who had my glasses but I knew I was going to do what I had to do to find them.

The shot caller let me know that he didn't have anything to do with the theft and that he and some of his homies were trying to help me search. I didn't trust anybody at that point because usually the very same people who offer to help you search are the very same people who stole the stuff in the first place.

I was in a very dangerous situation; I was alone in the cell with ruthless gang members. I was scared, but I was madder than I was scared and I was prepared to fight everybody in that cell to get my glasses back.

I remembered this one brother who kept hanging around my bunk and he didn't sit well with me. I felt there was something suspicious about him, and something told me to check his bunk. I approached his bunk when I thought he wasn't around, and when I raised his mattress I found a few of my other things but not my glasses. I knew he didn't have much of anything when he came in so I knew these were my things.

I took my things back and as I turned around to leave, I was knocked off balance by a shot to the head and I dropped the few things I had taken from under his bunk. In situations like that, when one gang member begins to fight, everyone who is down with him generally jumps in. So when I got hit I just assumed I was being rat packed (jumped on).

When I received the blow to my head it blurred my already-blurred vision. So I began throwing punches in the air at every direction. I was wondering why my punches weren't connecting to anybody.

As my vision began to clear up a bit I realized there was nobody around me. I was in the center of the aisle throwing punches at nothing but air. Now, that's hilarious!

I could hear some of the inmates saying, "Ah, man, that's messed up; you know he can't see without his glasses." My heart was pumping and my adrenaline was flowing as I located the dude who hit me and stole my things, and probably my glasses. He was taking off his shirt and shouting his gang affiliation, "What's up, Cuz! This is Grape Street Watts, Cuz!"

Usually when this happens the other Crips would join in solidarity and they would attack, but this time none of the other Crips moved. There was my jar of hair grease sitting in the middle of the aisle, which became the focal point. He claimed it was his and I knew it was mine. The grease wasn't so important but it symbolized a greater point.

I was breathing heavily and I was in a fighting stance. He was still trying to excite the rest of the Crips by taking off his shirt and hollering Crip, but they still didn't move. Every time he would try and pick up the jar of grease I inched closer and he would back up screaming "Crip!". Still, no one moved.

I could see fear in him. He was scared, all right. He was a distance away from the grease, still trying to excite the crowd. I saw he really didn't want a fair fight, so I walked over to the jar of grease and picked it up and turned my back on him and began to walk away.

I knew he was a coward, and I knew he would try and rush me from behind when my back was turned. As I walked away, I felt him coming at me. I never turned around but I ran a little ways and ducked behind a row of beds. I knew this would give him a false sense of security and bravery. He was feeling really good because he thought I was scared and that he had me on the run, but he was dead wrong.

He hit the corner at full speed and I cracked him in the head with the grease and I began to beat him senseless. I could hear the sheriffs coming and everyone made their way to their bunks. I was bleeding heavily because the jar had broken and cut the hand I hit him with, so I quickly wrapped it in the sheet. I was breathing heavily when the sheriffs walked by my bunk and looked at my blood-soaked sheet, and they kept right on walking.

I believe the sheriffs saw me having problems and they let me handle it on my own. Usually in a case like that they would have put me in the hole and that would be that.

When the sheriffs left, I began to gangbang on the entire dorm. At this point, whatever they had believed I was, their opinion of me quickly changed. I think they had believed I was soft. For just a moment I was the Crip I used to be. The shot caller carefully approached to calm me down. He wondered why I never said that I had a Crip background.

I explained to him that I had hung up my rag years ago. I wasn't gangbanging on the streets and I wasn't going to gangbang in jail for protection. I informed him that I would line them all up and get down with everyone of them if it meant my individuality.

I told him I couldn't understand how they could just let wannabes in their circle, just to increase their numbers. He agreed and made the dude get my glasses back, which by then were in another dorm with another inmate.

I had been down about four months fighting my case. They eventually transferred me to another LA county facility. I had been there before and it was a more comfortable environment where we had a little more freedom and we were allowed to go out in the yard.

I spent most of my time writing because that was my hustle. I would write poetry for inmates to send to their significant others, but what made the most money were the letters I would write to the judges for other inmates.

If you had any chance of getting out of jail, my letter to the judge would almost ensure it. Most inmates didn't know what a judge wanted to hear from them, so when the judge sentences an inmate in the county system they do it based on what they see or what they hear, which, of course, is mostly negative. So when the judges read my letters it was refreshing to them.

When I first began to write the letters for the inmates, the hater inmates talked about me, telling the inmates what I was doing wouldn't work. I couldn't refute it, because up to that point no one had gotten out because of my letters.

Three of the inmates felt it couldn't hurt and tried my letters to the judge. Other inmates were telling them that I was trying to hustle them and that they were wasting their money.

The inmates who purchased my letters went to court on the same day and got back at the same time. I was in chow hall when they came in, throwing up their hands to me. Two of them were about to get released and the other got considerable time knocked off of his sentence. I kept my head down like it wasn't nothing, but I felt really good inside.

After that, everyone was trying to get letters from me—even the haters. Many of them, with unrealistic expectations, wanted me to write a letter from them to the judge. One guy wanted me to write a letter to the judge that would get him out.

I had to tell him, "Look, man, you killed three people; there were several witnesses and they caught you with the gun at the scene."

He said to me, "Yeah, I know; so what do you think?"

So I'm at this other facility and they bring in this cat from prison who was fighting a case. He had been in prison for quite some time and came in with a sense of entitlement. I ran a store where I sold cigarettes, candy, etc. I sold out and my partner had a visit and I told him that I would watch his store. The prison dude tried to wrestle the store from me and I took it and put it under my bunk.

So I was writing more poems on the top of my bunk, which was the top bunk. The prison dude slept across from me and he kept staring me down, but I paid him no attention.

My partner comes back from his visit and gets his store and sits on the bottom bunk under me. I had my poems lined up neatly on my bunk and the prison dude came and laid his elbow on my nicely written sheet of paper. I politely asked him to remove his elbow from my papers.

He went back over to his bunk, talking stuff. I realized I was going to have to take care of this situation and I had to be prepared for what could happen. So I packed up my things and put everything in my blanket, in case something went down and the sheriffs came, so they could just grab my things in one big bundle and take me to the hole (solitary confinement).

Later, I went up to the guy in the day room and I told him that if he opened his mouth and said another disrespectful word to me I was going to handle him. I'm not sure what he said, but it was enough for me to let him have it. I beat his face in and then we heard the familiar sounds of the rumbling of sheriff's boots. I ran to my bunk, pulled out a newspaper, and was reading it when they hit the dorm.

They made everyone strip down to their underwear and sit on their bunks. The sheriffs were inside of their glass viewing room. The prison inmate came out of the day room, staggering to the window, and pressed his bloody face up against it and cried out for help.

They had us on that bunk for hours. Some of the inmates didn't know what happened because it went down so fast, but they wanted whoever was responsible to speak up. I would have but I found out that the big bad prison dude said three people had robbed him and beat him up, and I told them I wasn't going down for any jailhouse robbery.

As we were being checked for injuries, this one particular sheriff kept staring at me. I believe he knew it was me, but he also saw dude pressing up on me earlier. They finally let us off of our bunk and nothing came out of the situation.

I finally got sentenced. I took a three-year prison deal that ran concurrent with my three years joint suspension. Basically, I was going to get three years anyway because I violated my probation. My letter to the judge persuaded him to run both charges together for a total of three years and I said I would take it. I couldn't have gotten any less time but I could have gotten considerably more.

When you are sentenced to prison you are taken to a cell where you wait to be transferred to prison; this is called catching the chain. I still had my store and I was trying to sell as much as I could before I left.

These two dudes came up to me and asked me if I could sell them a pack of cigarettes for a discount price. I told them no, the price was the price. I really wasn't thinking, because I wasn't going to be able to take them to prison with me and I thought I needed to be tough. They then told me that I couldn't sell in the dorm anymore, and then stole some of my store that I had under my bunk.

So an old OG friend of mine saw me upset and asked me what was wrong. I told him what had happened and he was ready to go to war. He had 22-inch arms and his chest stuck out like he had been lifting weights all of his life. I didn't want to get him involved. I wasn't banging any more and I told him that I would handle it. He wasn't hearing what I was saying and told me to point out who was giving me trouble. When I pointed the dudes out, my OG's arms shrunk from 22 inches to 17 inches, and his chest shrunk too. He said, "Chuck, I can't help you, Cuz."

It just so happened that the cats I had trouble with were from one of the most notorious gangs in the United States, the Rolling 60s, and my big homie was no fool. Now I didn't want beef with any gang, especially the Rolling 60s. But I talked some mess anyway and kept selling my stuff.

That night I felt I was going to get hit (stabbed), so I fixed a knife made up of sharpened pencils and I lay in my bunk all night waiting for them to come, and then the lights popped on, and I heard my name, "Acrie, you're catching the chain!" That was the most beautiful sound I had ever heard. I was so happy to be going to prison; it meant I wasn't going to die in that cell.

The funny thing is I thought more about the incident than they did. They had been through this situation before, and it was all new to me. I wasn't a threat to them, and besides they had been smoking and eating candy on me all day anyway.

They transferred me to Susanville, a prison just on the California and Nevada boarder, but before I went there I went through a classification process where they sent me to Chino and then Donavan in San Diego.

I had never been to prison, so my eyes were wide opened. I wasn't scared, I was just going along with the program. I was no longer in control of my movements, what or when I ate, or where I slept. I had given all of those privileges up.

When I left Chino and went to Donavan in San Diego, California, it was a bit different. It was a newer prison and much different from Chino. They let us go out on the yard, so this was my first time seeing cats lifting weights. You always see dudes come out of prison with all of these muscles and I guess this is where it starts.

I looked around for some weights that I could handle. You have to realize: I was very tall, but I was very skinny. I saw two ten-pound dumbells and I began to workout with the weights. I must have looked crazy working out with those small weights because some of the younger cats were laughing at me.

Do you know how it feels when you lift weights and you overdo it the first time? Well, I did too many curls and the next morning my arms were stuck out by my side and it appeared that I was flexing my muscles.

Just imagine a real tall skinny man walking around like the Hulk with his arms in the flexing position. They started calling me, "Big Swole." It wasn't funny then but it's funny as heck now—okay, okay, it was funny then too. I was so embarrassed that when I got to Susanville I promised myself that I would never lift weights again.

When I got to Susanville, I was just happy to finally be at the place where I was going to finish my time, because your halftime didn't start until you got to where you were going to do your time. Back then, when you went to prison you would only have to do half of your time and then you were eligible for parole.

It was very cold outside, and when you are brought into prison you were just in a jump suit and karate shoes. You didn't even have underwear.

Some of the homies from Long Beach saw me and immediately tried to get me down to the weight pile, which, as you well know, I wasn't having any of it. When they finally let us into the dorms I was extremely tired. I took my bedding and began to make up my bunk. There was a little dude sitting on the bunk under mine.

Now let me tell you just how cold-blooded prison is. I was talking to the young guy; I could tell he was a young gangbanger so I began to tell him about my brief time as a gangbanger in Carson. The next thing you know I was talking to myself, because he was gone.

Ten minutes later a crowd of about twenty gangbangers from Carson approached me and asked me where I was from. I told them that I didn't bang but when I did it was in Carson. They began to tell me that they didn't know me and I could see they were trying to give me problems.

I began to give them a history lesson about the hood they were claiming. I began to name not only people they knew, but also people who they should have known. I was on a personal basis with some of the youngster's people. They quickly recognized that I was legit and changed their attitudes. They asked me where I lived, and I told them

Long Beach, but that I wasn't a part of a gang, and they quickly left me alone. I began to laugh because I had only heard about this kind of thing happening. It happened to me and I passed the test.

Ten minutes later, another group of about fifteen gangbangers from Long Beach approached me and told me they had heard that I was from Long Beach and asked where I was from; was I with the Insane or the 20s Crips. I told them that I didn't bang. They said that they hadn't heard of me and I could see they were going to give me problems, so I began dropping names and giving them a history lesson on the hood they were claiming. I told them I was sure that if they call their mommas and daddies they would tell them who I was.

Then, I asked the dude leading the pack where he was from, and he told me he had lived on 17th Street; I asked him if he knew Box and his face lit up. Then, I took a closer look at him and immediate recognition kicked in.

I said, "Man, you the youngster that Box sent to get me two ounces of cocaine from behind a trash can about nine months ago."

He looked at me and said, "Slim."

He recognized me. I was fortunate both times, because just like I told young dude in the county jail who had tried to rob me: you better hope they know who you are when you hit the yard.

I did finally hit the weights, and believe it or not I got swole. I had more muscles than I ever had, but it did nothing for my mind.

It was about eleven years between the time I went to prison for the first time and the next time. I had been in the entertainment business and hadn't liked the direction it was taking me, so I began to hustle with other hustlers. I was taught how to take the numbers off of legitimate checks and create dummy checks that would clear the bank.

I knew it was illegal but I also knew that it was a potential way of making money. When the entertainment business fizzled out for me, I decided that I would take a chance with these checks. I needed money and I was going to get it in the quickest and easiest way possible.

Just before that, I was hustling with another friend I had met in the entertainment business. We both had established a music production company that consisted of some talented rappers and producers, but my partner was a true hustler and he knew how to make money

He brought me in on a hustle called the take-backs. We would open up accounts under fictitious names, put money in the account on Friday, shop throughout the weekend, and take the money out of the bank first thing Monday morning before the stores were able to take their receipts to the bank. Then we would take the items back to the stores for refunds.

That hustle was safer but a bit too slow for me. I knew that creating checks would be quicker but a lot more dangerous. I was willing to take the risk.

What I would do is go around and make checks in the names of desperate people who didn't mind using their own IDs. I worked up and down I-65 making money.

When I was in Louisville, Kentucky, they were pretty dry as far as weed went. So I flew back to California and bought about six pounds of weed and shipped it back to where I was in Kentucky.

I hadn't done my homework, and the United States Postal Inspector got hold of my package and set me up. They had posted up several blocks away, with the FBI setting up a command post. When they delivered the package to me, something didn't feel right. I had my friend sign for the package in her own name so that she didn't look like she was part of the conspiracy.

I jumped into the truck and began to take wide circles around the neighborhood, trying to locate a command post if there was one. I let my greed take over and I popped open the package, which triggered the electronic device attached to it and the place was hit with an army of law enforcement officers from all over.

They informed me that if I had made one more circle they would have had to call it off because I would have run right into them. They gave me a state charge in the beginning and allowed me to bail out. When I got out, I immediately left Kentucky and went back to Long Beach, California.

I hadn't planned on going back to court and by then they had federally indicted me. Several months later I was pulled over and taken into federal custody. It's a trip when you are getting pulled over and you know there is no way out. I began to lightweight cry to myself, and then I began to laugh at myself because I sounded so ridiculous.

To see "your name vs. the United States of America" is a sobering feeling. I felt like, "What have I done to everybody in the United States of America?" I knew a few banks and a few corporations were angry with me, but the entire USA!

I was locked up at MDC Los Angeles, Metropolitan Detention Center. I was worried because I had got caught with a gun, the six pounds of weed, and the computer I was doing my white-collar stuff on. They had everything and I was afraid I was going to be put away for a very long time, and that's how they stacked my charges.

I was transported back to Kentucky to a small town called Litchfield. The jail housed federal inmates but it looked liked some kind of dungeon with safety and health concerns.

I walked into my cell, and the guy who would become my cellie was lying on his bunk, chilling. I was in some kind of way because while I was in MDC in Los Angeles, I found out they had this new law called 5k1.1; if you cooperated with the prosecution they would reduce your sentence at their discretion. I guess you could call it snitching with benefits.

I was tripping because so many people were getting down like that. What I've always heard was snitches get stitches, but it seemed that everyone was doing it and I was bothered by it.

So I began venting to my new cellie. I mentioned to him that I thought I would write a book about it, or a movie script. I began to break the story down to him from the beginning to the end. That's how I would create sometimes, by telling my vision to someone who had the time to listen; when it's going good I can possibly complete an entire project, and that's what happened.

When I was done rattling off this book concept, my cellie just sat up in his bunk with an amazed expression on his face. I thought he was looking like that because he thought my story was brilliant, like many do when I'm able to create in that fashion. But what I was to find out later was that he didn't necessarily think my story was brilliant; he was tripping because I was telling his story.

There were several other federal inmates in the jail from across the United States who thought Kentucky was a great place to commit crime. We all became cool with one another, so when we found out they were moving all of us to a new facility we devised a plan where we could all stay in the same dorm room.

We figured if we all claimed to need special diets we could stay in the same location, and it worked. There was a boxer and his cousin from New Jersey, a few cats from Kentucky, my old cellie who was from Florida, a gangster from Shoreline Crips in LA, and a few other guys from various parts of the US.

I had gotten pretty close to my old cellie, as well as the rest of the guys who transferred to the new facility. We were all away from our home states, except for a couple of us. We passed the time away by playing card games, chess, and talking about sports and politics. We worked on our cases because we all had cases pending and all of them were pretty big cases.

The gangster from LA had an upcoming court date. My old cellie was like a jailhouse lawyer and he helped people with their cases. The young gangster had his paperwork spread all over the tables in the twelve-man cell. I expressed to the young man that he should be more careful with exposing his case like that; although we were all close, we weren't that close.

In his case, he and his nephew were transporting a key of cocaine and they dumped it when they realized the police were trailing them. The cops found the dope and the two of them were arrested. The nephew beat the case and they had a hung jury on my young gangster friend, but they had re-filed on him and once again it was his day in court.

When I told him to keep his case closer to his vest because he was too close to beating the case, he said to me, "Ah, Cuz, we all family in here, Cuz! I got this, Cuz; they ain't got nothing on me."

When he went off to court, so did my old cellie. A few weeks later we got a kite (a note) from the young gangster from Shoreline Crip and what he told us gut punched us in the most horrible way.

My old cellie, after leaving our cell, made a call to the district attorney that was on the gangster's case and gave him the information that kept the prosecution from a conviction in the first case. The young gangster was eventually sentenced to life in federal prison without the possibility of parole.

That's why my old cellie looked at me when I told him about the book I was going to write. I had told his story all the way down to the letter, because that is what my story was about: a jailhouse lawyer who helped inmates with their cases but had an agreement with the federal prosecutions office to set up unsuspecting inmates. My script is entitled *Downward Departure*.

My old cellie was so pissed off when I called and told his woman about what he had done. We were that close. This dude was so bold that when he was flown back in to testify against the young gangster he requested to be put back in our cell, even though he knew we were well informed that he was a snitch. I didn't really get it.

We were asked as a unit if we wanted him back into our cell and we told them absolutely not. One day, he was being walked past our cell and for some reason our cell was open. He and I began a verbal assault on one another and I headed out of the cell to get at him. My other cellmate, the boxer, ran and grabbed me.

"That's what he wants you to do. That's why he came back!" the boxer told me.

I found out just how conniving that snitch was. When he found out that I had contacted his woman he decided to come back and try to get into our cell, knowing that he would be assaulted. What I also found out is that if you assault someone who is under 5k1.1, a contracted snitch, you automatically get five additional years on top of any sentence you were getting.

We organized an Alcoholic and Narcotics Anonymous program for federal inmates at the facility every Tuesday, but we refused to be let out of our cells as long as that snitch was out there.

All of the time he was down, he always bragged about how big time he was and all of the things he had. The guy who brought back the kite told us that he was dressed in an old, played-out looking suit. He was a bum in every sense of the word. Being locked in federal prison is just like being on Facebook: you can pretend to be anything you want.

I was still fighting my case. I spent a great deal of time in the law library learning criminal law as it applied to me. They tried to offer me the 5k1.1 but I flatly declined. Even if I wanted to tell on someone I couldn't think of anyone I hated enough, and besides, I just wasn't built like that.

It was really scary going into federal court. The way my charges were stacked, it seemed they were trying to give me over forty years. The more I spent in the law library the more I learned what the federal government could do to me, and what they couldn't do to me. What I also learned was how many cats were snitching under the 5k1.1 statute.

One of the first cardinal rules about jail and prison is that you don't snitch; if you snitch, you die. This was a different time, a different era. It seemed that everyone was trying to get a deal those days.

You wouldn't believe how much the coldest and hardest gangsters I've ever seen were telling on each other.

Fighting cases on the state level is a far cry different from fighting cases on the federal level. There was a time when being indicted by the feds meant you were fighting a white-collar case: bank fraud, wire fraud, some kind of fraud. I believe the federal government was seeing how much money the state was making off of the crack cocaine boom and the conspiracy that prompted it, and the feds wanted their cut. So the feds began picking up state cases, which changed the dynamic of federal prison life.

Now, the feds were picking up state cases under federal law, but the young men they were prosecuting were still under the same ideology of the state process. This meant that when the state prosecuted you they offered you a deal. It was customary to turn down the first deal because everyone knew you had to wait the prosecution out because they were sure to come down until you got the deal you desired.

Now that's fine at the state level, but at the federal level it's a bit different. When the federal government offers you a deal and you don't take it, they will go up the next time you go to court. So if they offer you five years and you don't take it, when you come back to court it may be ten years.

The thing that is so crazy to me was seeing all of those young men who went into the federal system unprepared. They would come in gangbanging, many of them, playing games and watching television, while the federal government did what they do best: put people away at the rate of 94 percent.

These young men came into the federal system with a state system frame of mind, and they were being eaten up by the thousands. They misunderstood how the federal system worked and they were taking deals that really weren't deals at all. They didn't do their homework.

There was this young man who was offered a five-year deal. The young man felt that five years was an adequate time to do for the crime he allegedly committed. He came back to the cell extremely happy. He bragged about the deal he had received; he called his friends and family. Two weeks later when he came back from getting sentenced; he was crying and shaking uncontrollably.

What happened was he actually received fifteen years in prison. What he didn't know was that he did get the five years for the offense, but he got an additional ten years for his criminal history. What these youngsters didn't know was that when you are sentenced for your criminal offense, you also get points for your criminal history, and if you have a lengthy criminal history you will also have a lengthy federal prison sentence.

Inmates began coming to me for advice because they saw how diligently I was working on my case. What I read in the paperwork of the men who asked for my assistance was disheartening.

There were so many people snitching; it was crazy! Inmates began to realize the federal government was not playing around and they were giving out lifelong sentences.

One day, it was time for me to go to court. I discussed with my federal defender what I wanted done. When I entered the courtroom he was late and hadn't done anything I had asked him to do. Actually, he didn't have to do anything but do as I instructed. I had reviewed my case and checked out case laws and statutes that paralleled with my case, but he wanted to do what he wanted to do, which was nothing.

When I got in front of the judge I asked for my attorney be recused (removed). The judge refused and the attorney wouldn't recuse himself, so for a minute I was stuck. I decided to write a heartfelt letter to my attorney. I broke him down in such a way that he became insulted and recused himself.

I received another attorney and he did exactly what I asked him to do. I handed him my case file with all of my research and asked him to do as I instructed. He read over what I had compiled for myself and began to laugh. He told me that I was in the wrong profession.

On the day I went to court, he presented to the judge exactly what I had presented to him and the judge reduced my sentence by nine months without snitching. I was sentenced to five years, minus the nine months.

Just like the state prison system there was a classification process. This process took place in Oklahoma. The marshals escorted us to a huge plane they called Conair and it was surrounded by about twenty heavily armed US Marshals. When we arrived in Oklahoma we pulled right up to the prison and we walked right in from the plane. It was like an airport.

Although I was busted in Kentucky, they sent me close to home, to a facility called Lompoc near Santa Barbara, California. There is always a feeling of relief when you get to where you are going because that is when your actual time begins.

In the lower level, which is FCI, or Federal Correctional Institution, it's pretty laid back, but you can bet your bottom dollar there are a lot of snitches there. I had been down for about a year when I was called to roll it up. I didn't understand why they had told me to roll it up because I still had a few years left on my sentence.

They told me that Kentucky had come to get me and they didn't know why. I was put into jeans, a t-shirt, my sneakers, and a hoodie, where I stuck my hands in the pockets that had holes in them and they cuffed me from the inside and zipped my hoodie up. They did this so that the people who flew on the plane didn't see my hands cuffed. It just looked like my hands were in my hoodie pockets. They were going for that natural look because we were riding on a commercial flight.

When I got there I found out that when I had first been arrested in Kentucky it had been a state case and that the case was never cleared off of their books. I stayed there for a month under the most horrible conditions—not as bad as the LA county jail but it was bad enough.

When I finally got into court, the judge dismissed my case because I was already doing time for the same crime. I couldn't wait to be called to go back to Lompoc.

Aside from the stay in the Louisville County Jail, my time away from Lompoc was okay. I had eaten McDonalds and things like that, so it was cool. I hadn't had outside food for some time.

When I got back to Lompoc I waited in the front to be let in. Something was very eerie about the place, but I couldn't put my finger on it. When I got into the gate I knew something was going on but I still didn't know what. Nobody was speaking to me. Then one of the inmates came up to me, telling me that I had a snitch jacket put on me and people were talking.

Now this is a very serious situation and I was wondering what was going to happen next. What was supposed to happen was that the people making the accusations were supposed to come with proof and then they would have me removed from the yard or worse. That's the prison code.

This was the rumor that was going around about me: two men came in black suits, and I was taken out in a black suit. My hands were free and I got into a long stretch limo where I was taken to a helicopter. I then flew to a private air strip where I boarded a private jet that took me to Columbia, where I testified against the Medellin Cartel and then was taken to a plastic surgeon where they were going to change my total appearance, so that Chuck Acrie would never be seen again." That's how crazy it was.

When people believe you are snitch in prison you are supposed to be rolled up and put off of the yard by the inmates. I wondered why they weren't handling their business. I was pissed because they are treating me like a snitch but nobody was making a move. It wasn't making any sense to me.

So it stood to reason why everyone was tripping so hard when they saw me. I reached out to one of my homeboys from Long Beach and approached him with my paperwork. I also talked to a group of concerned cats and told them that I would show them my paperwork to clear everything up. Well, they were pretty happy for me to show them my paperwork, but I wasn't finished. I said, "I'll show you mine when you show me yours." Everything went kind of silent. Some were cool with it but you could tell others weren't happy about it at all.

So I suggested we have a PSR (pre-sentencing report) party. Everyone knows that if you are a snitch it will be in your pre-sentencing report. Next thing you know the word got back to the warden and he made everyone turn in or throw away their PSR; you would go to the segregation unit if they found out you still had one.

Some of the snitches were scared and knew they would be exposed and they made that trip to the warden. We never had the PSR party. Most believed my story, but although there were some who wanted to believe that I was a snitch, nobody messed with me and they all respected me.

There is one thing you can never get back and that's time. Once it's gone you will never see it again. When you sit around discussing the past with friends and family and they begin to talk about things you should know but instead there is a big blank, it is so difficult.

To the Kids/Inmates/Future Inmates:

Some of you think this jail thing is a joke until you end up there, looking at big time behind bars. When I was fighting my federal case I saw some of the hardest gangsters and criminals cry like babies when they were being sentenced to all of that time. In the feds, your time is calculated by months. I saw cats being sentenced to over two hundred, three hundred, four hundred months of time in prison. That's a long time.

You have to do 85 percent of your times in the feds instead of doing 50 percent of the time in the state. There is nothing cool about jail or prison. Prison is a multibillion-dollar business. The people who own these prisons, and the for-profit businesses associated with these prisons, continue to get filthy rich off of our ignorance and the unfair laws that keep you locked up.

If you are a teenager and you are in a situation where you have to make a decision whether or not to get involved with drugs, gangs or crime, **JUST SAY NO!** Once you say yes to the things that will take you in the direction of drugs, gangs, and crime you are preparing to go to jail. They have a place for you, and if they don't they will make one for you.

If you haven't gone to jail, or if you haven't gotten into any real trouble in your life, and you are faced with the decision of doing anything that could potentially send you to jail, take the time, maybe a few minutes, to weigh out the consequences and make the right decision.

If you have done lengthy prison sentences, and you are in a situation where you have to make a decision that could get you caught up all over again, reflect back on your prior prison life and imagine having to go through all of that again and then do what's right. Just because you have done time in jail or prison doesn't make it the end of your life; it just may be the beginning.

I had to physically fight in jail. Any one of those situations could have ended my life, or I could have taken a life and never gotten out of prison. So don't think I'm glorifying fighting. I did what I had to do to survive. I should have never been in that situation in the first place.

To the Parents:

As a good parent you do all that you can do for your children. When they go out there and do what they want to do as opposed to what they are supposed to do it's on them. Of course it affects you, but you cannot put undue pressure on yourselves.

The kids these days are very smart, with a wealth of information at their disposal. If they do something that lands them in jail, be there for them as best you can but don't put added pressure on yourselves. Jail can be a learning experience that your child needs to see the error of their ways. They have to realize that there are consequences for their actions.

It all goes back to training that child to do what's right at an early age. It may not be 100 percent, but it can reduce the chances of your child landing in jail or doing big prison sentences.

If your child is an adult, allow that adult child to take his or her lumps. If you keep rescuing them, how can the lesson ever be learned?

A LEADER OF MEN

I was about twenty-five years old and I was absolutely in ruins. Crack had brought me so far down that I was only known as a crackhead. My girlfriend was pregnant and I needed to do something. I was sick and tired, but mostly sick. I was just ready for a better life.

I decided to join the army. I was a good cook, so that's what I went in as: an army cook. I was surprised they let me in because I was so sucked up. I was 6'6" and only weighed about 185 pounds. I looked horrible. I looked like the character Chris Rock played in New Jack City.

I got in and I headed off to basic training. Even though I was tore up they still saw the leadership potential in me and made me the platoon guide. Some of the other recruits felt they should have been the platoon guide because they had done ROTC in high school. One day they closed me in my room so that I couldn't hear the alarm, and when I wasn't out in front of the platoon the drill sergeants came looking for me.

When they saw me lying in my bunk they flipped out and threw my entire mattress out of the top floor window. If that wasn't bad enough, they made me get down and do pushups in front of the entire platoon. I only had ten in me, and when they tried to make me do more I fell flat on my face. There was a drill sergeant in each of my ears. They were calling me any and everything they could think of that wasn't good.

I was exposed. They knew my biggest weakness and they made sure they took advantage of that fact. They made me do pushups as a way of humiliating me—or so I thought at the time. There was another guy there—I believe he was from Philadelphia—and they would clown us together.

We came up with a plan. We decided to work out every night during lights out. One day they tried to clown us when the sergeants saw a platoon of women coming and decided to make my boy and I get down and do push-ups. They told us to do twenty pushups and to stand in the front- leaning rest position (the up position).

Usually, we would eventually cave in, but when we locked in the front-leaning rest position we leaned forward. The sergeants got mad and made us do twenty more. When we completed the twenty, we locked and then leaned again. The sergeant got upset and told us to get up. We didn't get up but stood right there, locked in the front-leaning rest position.

We looked liked two pit bulls. The sergeants got really angry with us but never made us get down to do push-ups again.

I've always had leadership potential, but that's just the thing—my potential always exceeded my accomplishments.

Those sergeants stayed in my behind. I had heard that when they think you are a good recruit they put extra pressure on you to see how much stress you can take without folding. All that being said, it felt personal to me. I guess I can honestly say I wasn't giving my all and I would do silly things sometimes.

Like one day we were out training and one of the rules was you don't pick up anything because there could be live ammo (ammunition) out there and it could potentially detonate. I was bored and I saw this old-looking ball thing on the ground and I picked it up. I began whistling the Globe Trotter theme song while I used this old-looking ball thing like a basketball and began rolling it up my arm and back down. I threw the thing over my shoulder and caught it behind my back.

I had a few of my troop members laughing and then I went over to one of the Sergeants and did the entire Globe Trotter routine with the little old-looking ball thing. The sergeant began to stutter.

"Pu—pu—pu—pu—pu—put that thing down," he said softly.

Acting silly, I said, "Wha—wha—wha—wha—wha—what did you say?"

He repeated what he said exactly like he said it before, stutter and all. He then said something that caught my attention: "It's a live hand grenade."

I quickly put the grenade down on the ground and moved away from it. The bomb squad was called in and had to detonate the thing. Of course, I was embarrassed. But they still had faith in me.

Even at the gun range, I would do silly things. I was in the prone position with my M-16 assault rifle aimed down range. I was minding my own business when this captain came and began to really get on me. I wasn't doing anything wrong. I was one of the best marksmen in my platoon, but he just kept on me and kept on me until I turned around and asked him what did he want. Unfortunately, when I swung around so did my M-16.

His eyes got as big as silver dollars and all you could here was him saying, "Down range! Down range!" I turned the M-16 back down range and kept shooting. One of my drill sergeants decided to pull me away and spoke to me in private. She broke everything down to me. She told me the reason they were on me so tough was because they saw me as one of the best recruits they had. She thought if she didn't tell me that I might really hurt somebody.

Believe it or not, I graduated from basic training and it was time for me to go to AIT (advanced individual training). Once again, I was made platoon guide. It seemed that every phase of training I entered I started off as platoon guide. I took this position very seriously. I was only an E-1 private, the lowest rank possible. There were soldiers who were higher ranking, and others who may have been more qualified, but the drill sergeant chose me.

Immediately, I gained the respect of my platoon. We didn't have to do much but drill in the morning and march to class after that. All we were required to do was go up and down the field, column right, column left, to the rear, and that's about it.

I just so happened to have in my platoon this young man who was a major in ROTC at his high school, and he specialized in drills. I put him in charge of teaching our platoon how to do all of those fancy routines they did at his school. My uniform was well pressed and my hat was well creased.

When we would go out to drill there would be about five other platoons out on the field. The distinction between my platoon and the rest of the platoons was like night and day. While all of the other platoons were going up and down the field, column rights and lefts, our platoon was doing all kinds of designs and routines. It looked as if we were preparing for a parade or the halftime of a football game.

I marched next to the platoon to make sure everything was in order. I had the ROTC young man on the other side giving instructions. I may have looked good and got all of the credit, but it was that young man who was making all of those beautiful movements happen.

One day, some high-ranking officers came to check things out with the various platoons. When they got out there and saw our platoon and what we were doing, and saw me marching around the platoon, all they said was, "Who is that?"

They came to the chow hall, and as my platoon waited in line they stood at parade rest (standing with your hands behind your back with your legs spread and your eyes faced front). When they moved up they would snap at attention, (arms to the side and feet together, with eyes faced front), move up, and snap back into parade rest at the same time. When the generals saw this they began to call me "Drill Private."

I loved the attention and my platoon loved the attention we were getting. I believe that our platoon drill sergeant didn't like the attention I was getting and he showed it. We were marching to class and I gave the command to go left. The sergeant scolded me and told me not to give any commands.

The next day, we were marching to class and when it was time for a command to turn left he didn't give one and I didn't give one either. I told the platoon to keep marching until I marched them right into a brick wall. He had told me not to give a command, so I didn't. Of course, my platoon was mad at me, and of course I was removed from platoon guide. I guess it was testosterone or something. I guess I did it to spite the sergeant, but all I did was make it hard on myself.

That wasn't even the worst part. When I was removed as platoon guide, I couldn't do the same things I required my platoon to do. I had gotten too big for myself. I was used to hanging with sergeants and I refused to stand at parade rest or any other thing. So now not only had I lost my position, but I lost the respect of my entire platoon.

I went on to complete my AIT and was stationed at Fort Hood, Texas. I can only tell you that it was all bad from there. I beat up a sergeant because he cut me with a knife and didn't apologize and I went street on him. That wasn't very smart. I got one dirty drug test and they didn' even want to wait for the other one to come back. They told me I didn't have to go home, but I had to get the heck out of the army.

They gave me an other than honorable discharge because they didn't want to waste any more time on me waiting for the second drug test to give me a dishonorable discharge.

I was so selfish. I had just gotten married and had a small child. I never thought that what I was doing was hurting my family. I was on something else. I was in the best place I could have been at that time. I totally ignored the fact that I was just months from being a crackhead.

To Everyone:

The lesson learned for me was that to be a great leader you must be a great follower. When I was dismissed from the platoon guide position in AIT, I should have been the first person to stand at parade rest and snap to attention. I should have led by example.

I didn't even stop to think how my platoon looked at me when I refused to do the things I had asked them to do. I didn't care what they thought; I was so selfish.

When you are put in a leadership position it comes with a great deal of responsibilities. You have to be willing to sacrifice for the sake of the team. You have to understand the people who are under you. You have to understand your own weaknesses. You have to listen to those under you.

To become a good leader, you must be a good follower. Leadership also begins at home. If you can't even lead your own family, how can you expect to be a leader of people?

That is what having character is all about: never putting you above the team and being a team player. I put myself above my platoon, but worst of all above my family. The true definitions of character are the sacrifices you make in life and taking care of your responsibilities.

DOGG POUND DREAMING

For as long as I can remember, I have wanted to be in some form of entertainment. I was born in Gary, Indiana, and lived down the street from the Jacksons when they formed the Jackson 5. My mother even bought me a guitar and had visions of the Jackson 5 becoming the Jackson 6. I know—funny, right?

When we moved to California I became a member of the Carson Community Players Performing Arts, where I performed in plays. I was also a pretty good writer. I wrote poetry throughout my high school years.

Once, I was in the library and I found a book of movies in script form. I saw the academy award-winning movie script, *On Golden Pawn*. I briefly scanned over the script and thought that I could do it.

I wrote my first script, entitled *Rock City*. It was the West Coast version of *New Jack City*. I've always been ahead of the trend but could never get my work looked at to see if I was good enough. I wrote *Rock City* a year before *New Jack City*. I wrote a script entitled *Modern Day Gangsta* two years before *Boyz In The Hood*.

I got with a local rapper named Domino I met at one of the plays I was a part of. He was brilliant and he had a hype man who was ridiculous, named Beefy. They asked me to come and check them out at the Roxy for a showcase they were performing at in Hollywood. They wowed the crowd and were by far the best act there. There were many record labels there and they were extremely interested in this act.

The problem was his music producer was accepting business cards, his producer's wife was accepting business cards, and his manager was accepting business cards. All three of them were contacting all of these labels at the same time, each trying to get a deal for Domino. This made it a problem and Domino was then blackballed.

What I came to realize was that the industry does not like problems; as soon as they recognize a problem, they will back off and it will spread to other music executives.

When he was at his worst, I introduced him to a friend of mine and had him, along with Beefy, perform for her. She was into real estate and I felt that since he was a seasoned act she could manage him.

She asked what I wanted and I said I wanted to do my movie and when he got his deal we could begin to pitch my script. Now how stupid was that? I should have asked for a percentage or something in writing, because as soon as they could they spun on me so fast it made my head spin.

I didn't tell my friend Domino had been blackballed and she tried everything to get him a deal but nothing happened. He performed on a compilation album under another name and eventually got a deal with a small record label. He came out with his first song and it was a hit: "The Ghetto Jam." The record was being played around the world.

They eventually came back to get me because my old friend wanted to get into the movie business and she knew I was the truth when it came to writing. Nothing ever came out of it. I wasn't treated as I should have been and I eventually moved on.

About this time Snoop was blossoming as well, and Dr. Dre and Death Row were truly on the map. One day, I ran into someone I knew who was the little brother of a really good friend of mine, C-Style. He just so happened to be Snoop Dogg's right hand man. I showed him my script and he showed it to Snoop. That's how I became affiliated with The Dogg Pound. They had a lot of music but they didn't have a movie script.

It was the beginning of Snoop's career and he was soaring. I was privileged to be a part of that entire experience. I was where I wanted to be, so all I thought I had to do was be a good person and treat people the way that I wanted to be treated. I wanted to lead by example. What in the heck was I thinking?

I was dealing with gangsters with gangster mentalities when it came to doing business. I was in the middle of it but I didn't quite understand it. On top of that, I wasn't on top of my business. Yes, I had a script, but I was actually clueless when it came to the entertainment business, and I didn't take the time to learn it. I took the easy road figuring it would happen because someone else would make sure that it did. I was too busy getting high and having fun.

I wasn't in awe of all of the celebrities I was privy to because I felt that I belonged. There was a false sense of security because being around these people made you feel that you were close to hitting it big, especially if you had talent.

When Suge Knight made that now-infamous statement on the stage against Puffy at the Source Awards in New York at Madison Square Garden, it was my first time in New York. At that time there was no East Coast/West Coast beef. But after Suge said what he said that night at Madison Square Garden, it kind of set the stage.

I was sitting in the third row, totally oblivious to what was going on. The entire place was chanting "EAST COAST"; We knew it was time to go. So we ended up leaving the show and headed to the after party.

I was in the VIP area enjoying the night when the guy who managed Death Row/Can Am Studio approached me and asked if I could knock a ninja out. This question confused me, but I followed him anyway because I thought our crew was in trouble.

As we were exiting the VIP area, he stopped abruptly as Suge and Puffy came into the area. The expression on the face of the man who came to get me spoke of me possibly knocking out Puffy, which I thought was ridiculous.

Suge and Puffy walked to the back; the music was blaring so the two of them had to talk into each other's ears. After about five minutes Suge walked casually toward us as Puffy walked casually out of the VIP area with his boys. Suge said, "We got to get out of here; round up everybody and let's go!"

I really don't know what was said but I could only assume that Puffy told Suge that this wasn't Los Angeles and that he ran New York and we had ten minutes to get out of there. Like I said, I didn't hear anything, but that's what it looked like to me, because we got out of there in a hurry.

When I got to the door all of the limos had gone and only Kurupt and I were left. We were surrounded by hundreds of people who recognized the King Pin and suddenly all of these wannnabe rappers were trying to rap against Kurupt.

It got to be too crazy, so I pushed Kurupt toward an open space and we walked down a street in downtown Manhattan with the crowd following closely behind us. A limo finally saw us and swung around to pick us up. We weren't worried because the East Coast/West Coast beef hadn't begun yet.

Dr. Dre began to expand his business and began to direct music videos and he wanted to direct and produce feature films. He had been in search of a script but at the time hadn't found one to his liking, or the liking of the executives at Interscope.

Snoop had my script but he was in no way in a position to get involved in the movie business because he was riding high on the music business. He put me in contact with Dr. Dre and Dre asked that I meet him at his spot on Wilshire Blvd.

I was really excited. I didn't have a car so I had to catch the bus from Long Beach to the Wilshire District. On the bus, all I could think of was that this could be it for me, the break I had been praying for.

When I walked inside of Dre's spot the excitement I felt quickly left me. Surrounding his entire apartment were stacks of scripts. I hadn't thought there could be other scripts there; that's not how I envisioned it.

Dre and I sat at the table and I pitched my script, *Modern Day Gangsta,* to him. After I was finished he was excited. He and I jumped into his Mercedes 600 and went directly to Interscope. When I got there I was introduced to Jimmy Iovine, the billionaire, and Interscope owner Ted Fields.

Dre and Jimmy went to one part of the office while Ted sat with my script in his hand; he began to read through it. Understand, I was just a novice and had never had anyone professionally look at my script, and now here I was, sitting with the man who signs the checks.

As Ted flipped through my script, he would look up with a strange look on his face. I believed he felt the script was probably amateurish but he was looking through it as a favor to Dre.

He shut the script after about twenty minutes and asked Dre when he wanted to shoot the movie. Dre looked up astonishingly and said, "You're kidding me." I guess Dre was surprised, because up to that point Ted had rejected all of the other scripts Dre had presented to him.

Dr. Dre and I left the Interscope office and we went to dinner to discuss the shooting of *Modern Day Gangsta.*

At this point I was in total elation because it appeared that my dreams were finally coming true. I was sitting and eating crab, lobster, steak, and all of the fixings with Dr. Dre, discussing the development of my script.

I was so excited I began to explain to him my ideas for the movie. I had written this song, "How Long Will It Last," and I thought it would go perfect with the movie. I began to sing the song to Dre. He stopped eating abruptly and said, "n*&^a, I didn't ask you to sing!" Have you ever gotten embarrassed and it got really hot? That's how I felt. Once again, hilarious!

For a minute I was allowed on the sets of a few music videos because I wanted to learn the business.

Unfortunately, from what I've been told, Suge went to Dre's house in Calabasas with some cats and confronted him about some business issues and I believe that was the last straw.

We stopped seeing Dre around the Can Am Studio. Dre decided to leave Death Row and create his own label apart from Suge. For a time he didn't want to have anything to do with anyone from Death Row or The Dogg Pound; I haven't seen Dre' since. I really liked Dre, and I can only imagine what would have happened if we would have remained in contact.

I stayed around the studio, hoping that I would get a break. I went to meetings with my script in hand. There is nothing like going into meetings and dealing with the CEOs of companies. Going in with Dr. Dre, I didn't need anything but a script; trying to go into places without a known name was difficult.

I eventually got into the music aspect of the entertainment business, singing hooks for some of the Death Row artists. I had a friend who was an amazing producer and a gifted singer, Darryl, but all he did was hang in his makeshift studio in his garage.

One day I had to literally force him out of his garage and I took him to the Death Row studio, Can Am. When we got there Snoop had this beat on and asked me to write something to it. Big Pimpin came up with the hook: Dirty Hoes Draws.

I had no problem writing the first sixteen bars of the song; I figured Nate Dogg would sing it. Snoop came in and asked me if I had finished and I said yes. Then he told me that I was on deck. Now, I didn't know exactly what he meant, but I hoped he didn't mean what

I thought he meant and wanted me to sing.

That's exactly what he wanted me to do. Sometimes Snoop and I would sing oldies but goodies together, and he knew I had a piece of voice, but I had never sung in a studio before and I immediately began to panic. At that point, there were only a few of us in the studio and none of them were singers except for my boy who I had brought out of his garage, Darryl.

I turned to him and asked him if he would sing the lyrics that I had written and he quickly told me no. He had an amazing voice and I couldn't understand why he wouldn't sing. So, reluctantly, I went into the sound booth and tried to sing the song. The next thing you know everybody came into the studio.

I was sweating bullets. It took me forever to sing those lyrics, but I finally did it and they came out pretty good—good enough to be put on Nate Dogg's first album.

I introduced Darryl, who I had brought up to the studio, to everyone there and gave him access to the studio whenever he wanted to come up there. One day, Suge Knight and I were talking and he said he liked Darryl and asked why I didn't represent him in the negotiation process. When I suggested it to Darryl he declined and went around my back and secured his own deal, totally distancing himself from me.

He went on to do music for all of the big names at Death Row, including Tupac. He came back years later and apologized, but it was what it was. Everybody comes back when the music stops. I don't know what makes people act and react to a little fame to the point that they lose their minds.

I was working on a project while Snoop was on trial for murder. The guy that I was working with was C-Style, Snoop's right-hand man at the time. I eventually became C-Style's right-hand man. He was the one who brought me into the Dogg Pound Family.

By the time the project was over I had befriended one of the artists, working with her and putting her on hot tracks. I called her on the night we were supposed to get paid. We were all meeting over at Snoop's house so I called her to make sure she didn't miss out.

When she got there she didn't really speak to me, but what she did was slide under Style and told him that I was trying to backstab him. She was so concerned she wasn't going to get paid; she felt she had to hedge her bet and throw me under the bus.

The thing that disappointed me the most, after all I had done for and with Style, was that he didn't think enough of me to talk to me about it. He just took her word. I never got paid.

I eventually hooked up with my boy Steve, and at the time he was the weed man and he was always about his money. Well, Steve had gotten into it with Style before and the fact that he and I joined forces—of course this didn't make Style too happy. We made amazing music and it was getting attention around the Death Row camp.

One day I was in the trailer at a Dogg Pound video shoot. My music was put into the player and everyone went crazy over it. They kept trying to find out whose music it was, and when someone said it was my music, everyone looked in stunned disbelief, because I wasn't really known for making music.

One day, we had a Dogg Pound meeting at Tray Deee's house. Everyone was there and C-Style came in with two of my rappers who I had signed to his label, J-Money and McGruff. I was also in a relationship with their mother, Jeanette. When he saw me, he immediately began to press up on me.

He sat next to me and tried to go into my pockets and told me that he was going to rob my business partner and me whenever he saw us in the streets. Everyone thought I was scared. I wasn't, I was just trying to figure out how I was going to kill him and get away with it, because at the time, I didn't see any other way.

Tray Deee was a gangster and he and I had gotten close. He came and did amazing songs on our compilation album. He was embarrassed for me and didn't want to hang around with anyone who was perceived as soft.

When I got up to walk out I knew I wasn't going to leave without dealing with C-Style. I kneeled next to him and asked him why was he messing with me. He stood up and we went at it, right in Tray Deee living room. It was crazy because he was like my little brother; I loved him like that and I couldn't understand after all of the loyalty I had displayed why it had to go down like that.

We were tearing Tray Deee's living room up. He was hollering, trying to get us out of his house and into the backyard. Daz Dillenger ran to his vehicle to get the video camera. Snoop was trying to protect the weed, and everyone else was just tripping.

C-Style and I were locked up on Tray Deee's couch. I was keeping my eyes on Style's henchmen, because I didn't trust anybody at that point.

This split Long Beach in half, with half of the people happy that it went down and the other half were riding with him and wanted to kill me. We eventually squashed it but we were never the same. He still never paid me, but he never disrespected me again either.

Kurupt asked me to come to Can Am Studio to put a hook on his song. We heard Suge had bailed Tupac out and he was doing music at Can Am while we were at a studio, Sound Castle in Glendale.

When I got there I went into studio A. Tupac was recording and when I walked in he quickly turned the music down and backed up, moving from side to side.

When I asked him where Kurupt was he said he wasn't there. It was a crazy feeling, and as I began to walk out, I forgot I needed to talk to him about my script Modern Day Gangsta.

He had turned the music back up and when I turned around he turned the music back down and backed up again, like he was preparing for a problem. I just said forget it and walked out.

Several weeks later, one of my producer buddies L.T. Hutton was working on a track with Tupac and asked me to come down to Can Am. When I went in, Tupac immediately got frustrated and told L.T. that he hadn't brought any of his homeboys to the session, so why had he? L.T. told Tupac who I was and that I was supposed to be there and that he was the new cat and to stop tripping.

Tupac completed his track and we sat down and chatted for a bit. He explained to me that after he had gotten shot in NY his trust level was very low and he apologized to me. He said he would love to do my movie but several months later he was dead.

After that I became so frustrated with the entertainment industry that I just began to make my money any way that I could, and of course the quickest way possible.

To The Kids:

Chasing your dreams is never a problem, as long as you go about it the right way. There are steps to take when you are a child that you cannot get around. Your education is top priority. Your dreams should start right there.

Set goals for yourself: small, medium and then long-term goals. Be practical and don't make unreasonable goals because you will run into major disappointments that will kill your dreams.

Don't be discouraged when your goals don't come together right away, just keep on developing and never give up.

Make sure you are prepared when an opportunity comes your way. There is nothing worse than a blown opportunity because you were not prepared. You can never get a second chance at making a good first impression.

To The Parents:

Support your children's dreams. Encourage them to reach beyond their own understanding. Take them to plays, concerts and other events.

The worst thing you can do is not be involved in their extracurricular activities. Motivate them and then support them. I wasn't there for my children's activities and there is a hollow feeling that I have inside because of it. It doesn't matter what I do for them now; I missed the most important times in their development.

Although they may not say as much, I know that it affects them to this day. There is no way you can get lost time back. Once it's gone, it's gone forever.

MY TURNAROUND

When I got out of the feds, I wasn't sure what I wanted to do. I really didn't have any formal skills and I didn't think school was the ticket for me either. I was released to my sister's house in Norco, California. That's North Corona for those of you who are unfamiliar with the name.

My sister, Gloria, and her husband, Ira, and his two kids lived in a very spacious and beautiful house. My mother also lived there but something wasn't right about her. When I was about to be released from prison, I would call my sister's house and my mother would have difficulty answering the phone. I knew something was wrong but no one would tell me what was going on.

My mother was suffering from dementia. For those of you who don't know what dementia is, it's like Alzheimer's, where you begin to lose your memory and cognition. At one point, my mother thought she was still working at one of her old jobs. She prepared for work one day and my brother-in-law, Ira, followed her and walked with her before convincing her to come back to the house.

I felt hopeless and didn't know what to do. Here I was trying to figure out my life after prison and I was faced with a situation I wasn't equipped or prepared for. To make matters worse, my sister had been diagnosed with multiple sclerosis (MS) some years ago, a debilitating disease that attacks your muscles and central nervous system.

My sister began displaying early signs. She had difficulty driving, and she was having trouble walking and balancing. I had probation restrictions, drug testing, finding a job, etc. to deal with, and I was in the middle of my sister and my mother trying to deal with their medical conditions.

Ira was working and it just wasn't in him to have to deal with these types of problems beyond the financial aspects; even that, after awhile, was taxing.

I kept hoping my mother would get better, but that never happened. My little brother, Sterling, couldn't handle seeing his mother and sister like that, so assistance was limited to me. The pain in my heart ran so deeply because I really loved my mother and sister and it was such a helpless feeling.

It seemed that my mother's condition and the condition of my sister worsened simultaneously. One moment my sister was walking and the next moment she wasn't. My mother refused to bathe and I found out that people suffering from dementia didn't like to bathe.

It was 2005 and by this time she had to be placed in a facility for her own safety. My mother's condition took a sudden turn for the worse. She was placed in the hospital and would eventually be put on life support. My mother was one of the most beautiful people, and man could that woman draw. I failed her in so many ways, and for the rest of my life that will haunt me.

I finally had to make the decision whether or not to take her off of life support. There was nothing else I could do; there was nothing anyone could do at that point. I made the decision to have her removed from life support and Ira and I watched her take her last breath.

By this time, my sister was pretty much confined to her bed. Now this was my younger sister, two years younger than me, and she couldn't walk anymore. For a moment, she just needed help to go to the restroom, until she just couldn't stand anymore.

Here I was a caregiver to my sister, a job I took extremely seriously because no one else could deal with that situation. I had to change my sister's Depends (diapers) and give her a bath and carry her up and down the stairs. I wasn't qualified to do any of these things but I was more than willing.

I used to play games with her, especially when it was time to change her Depends. It was already awkward, so I just made it fun. I remember one day I was changing her. I had just gotten her all cleaned up, and as I was getting ready to close the diaper she started doing the number two and it was huge.

At first, I started telling her off because I said she had done it on purpose, and then when I saw the size of that thing I began to run around the room, screaming at the top of my lungs like I had just seen a monster. She was laughing so hard, watching me act silly.

Finally, she had to be put into a facility because that was the only way she was going to get the care she needed. I would still go to her room and act silly. Her face would light up when she would see me. I made up a singing group call "Chuck And The Chuckettes." I used the nurses to join in the fun; my sister loved when I did that.

On the night my mother died, I went out to a club and began to drink and ran into an old flame. They call her Chocolate. It was good to see her, because at that moment it was all bad for me. She looked out for me through those trying times and I will never forget her for that.

I had some relationships in my life, but they were never healthy ones, and that was mainly because of me. It was due to a lack of responsibility and my own understanding of what I believed a relationship was all about.

It really wasn't fair to these women, because although I meant well, in many cases I never really took the relationships as seriously as

I should have, and then I was still trying to establish my own identity.

I was never really faithful and I had a hidden disrespect for the women who I called my own. It took me a long time to figure it all out, and it took Chocolate to bring it out of me.

The one thing I can say is that she gave me a run for my money. When our relationship ended in the early 90s she placed the number of a woman in my pager. Knowing the womanizer I was, she knew I would take the bait. I called the number she had left in my pager, and of course I charmed my way into the woman's life.

Now, Chocolate kept tabs on me, and the girl, not knowing she was being played like a flute, would give Chocolate all of the details. What I didn't know was that the girl had dealt with a guy Chocolate was involved with and she wanted her to stay away from him, so she used me to make that happen.

Men can say what they want but when it comes to deception, women are the absolute best.

I eventually decided that I would get into photography and videography as a career choice. I contacted an old friend of mine who is more like a brother to me, Dwayne. He played on my high school basketball team at Lakewood High School. As a matter of fact, I was the one who recruited him to come to my school.

He had become very successful in business and he slid me $10,000 and bought me one of those high-end video cameras. I began to shoot weddings and I attempted to produce two documentaries but it was more complicated than I thought it was going to be.

Dwayne turned me onto a friend, Ron Hightower, who went from porn star to becoming a successful director, producer, and editor, and he taught me editing and shooting the correct way. We shot a K-Ci from Jodeci solo music single video. Then I directed a TV reality show pilot, *The Trac Pack*, about a group of teen kids ready to venture out on their own to pursue their dreams without their parents.

Chocolate and I became a real couple, going through our share of ups and downs. She decided that she wanted to take a crack at comedy again and I got behind her on that. She is totally hilarious and she has taken the comedy world by storm. Coincidentally, that's her stage name: Comedian Chocolate Storm.

I really learned about being in a committed relationship from her. I wasn't faithful all of the time and she stuck in there with me despite.

I had lost contact with Dwayne. I heard he and Evander Holyfield were somewhere down south and had started a church. Not true, but that's what I heard. When I contacted him we got together because he wanted me to write some TV scripts for him but he had also got involved with this energy company, iCeL.

He told me how much money he planned to make and I wanted in on that. He wanted me to just focus on the entertainment aspect of the business and leave the energy business to him. Once he had to go out of town and I was in charge of his part of the energy business and the entertainment business. We were in the middle of editing the TV reality show as well as partnering up with this old guy that actually owned the energy company.

While Dwayne was gone I made myself a position in the energy company and got real close to the owner. When Dwayne got back in town all he could do was laugh. I eventually became the director of operations for the company, making pretty good money.

Chocolate and I got married and had a beautiful wedding. It was absolutely one of the happiest times in my life. I felt more responsible than any other time in all of my life. I was a husband in the truest sense of the word and I liked how it felt. This was my second marriage; the first time I really wasn't ready.

Chocolate was a beautiful bride. Mostly everyone was there who we cared anything about, including my father. Well, I told you that my father and I hadn't gotten along for some time. I was mad at him because he wouldn't loan me money to get a car when I got out of federal prison. We didn't speak for years; I only needed $300.

I thought I had a reasonable argument against him until I really sat down and thought about things. We never really got along but he never turned me away, and I had stolen from him when I was a crackhead.

It's funny, when you come back from being a crackhead, you forget some of the cold-blooded things you did to people, and you expect them to forget, too. My father didn't owe me anything, and I had the nerve to be mad at him. If anything, I owed him and he could have still been mad at me.

I reached out to my father and apologized to him. We began to hang out at some of my nephew's high school football games. I watched him get really involved with this young man's football career. This was his wife's daughter, Londi's son, but you couldn't tell they weren't related by blood.

Sometimes I thought how nice it would have been if he had showed that kind of interest in me when I was growing up, but then I had to think. This young man, Xavier, had impeccable character and good grades—things I had none of. He did all of the things he was supposed to do and I found myself rooting for him as well.

My father was a womanizer in his day, but when he found his true love, Lavon, he changed in so many ways. He treated her kids like they were his own. The youngest, Eric, was more of a son to him than I was. I began to go and see him and spend time with him. We began to get along like never before and I enjoyed it.

My kids and I are still pretty distant and I hope one day they can forgive me enough to communicate with me like I have been able to with my father. I hate that I wasted so much time away from my children.

The energy company, iCeL, went under because of mismanagement by the controlling owners. It was only because of my relationship with Dwayne that I had held such a position.

I didn't know what I was going to do after the failure of iCeL. No one was going to hire me and pay me what I had made at iCeL, especially because of my criminal history.

I came up with a plan to create my own company, a nonprofit. I took the name of an idea my wife, Chocolate, had for a dormant project and began to develop the company. Now, understand this wasn't bringing in any money, and it put a big strain on our marriage.

One day, I was driving down the street in my 745Li BMW feeling really good about myself and how things were going with my new company when I received a call from Walmart. I didn't know what they wanted but I was curious; I figured it was about some kind of gift card or something.

The lady on the phone asked me what day I wanted to come in for an interview. I was stunned because I hadn't applied for a position at Walmart. I didn't necessarily want a job at Walmart because I felt it was beneath me, but I scheduled the interview anyway. I rolled around in my car, thinking how that could have happened. I never applied to Walmart. Then, it all hit me like a sledgehammer, "MY WIFE!" I was upset, but not really. It wasn't like I didn't need a paying job.

While I was riding around, broke and with overinflated ideas of myself, preparing for future earnings, my wife had been at home submitting applications for me to get paid right now. I guess she felt I had amazing ideas but not one of them was paying any of the bills.

I eventually went to the interview and got the job at Walmart as a receiving associate, which means I was an unloader—a far cry from being the director of operations for iCeL Technology Solutions.

I was embarrassed about working for Walmart. I thought I was too good to work for Walmart. I thought people would look down on me, but it was just the opposite. People applauded me for doing what I had to do to provide for my family. It was a lesson learned late, but a lesson learned.

Most of the unloaders were young, in their early twenties. In the first two weeks I thought I was going to die. I wasn't used to working like that, and to add insult to injury I was a diabetic. It didn't take me very long to adjust to the heavy workload. I became healthier and I began to appreciate the opportunity Walmart had given me.

I never relinquished my goal of becoming a nonprofit; I continued to develop Heal Through Laughter. One of my other responsibilities was going to visit my sister. It was difficult seeing my little sister in a facility, but I put on a brave front for her. When I would walk into her room her face would light up.

It always hurt me so badly when I would leave there. Her quality of life was poor because her legs were contracted; she had to be fed through a feeding tube and she couldn't talk very well.

One evening, I received some of the worst news I could have imagined. My brother-in-law called to say that I needed to get to the hospital because my sister didn't have very long to live, and once again I was the one who needed to make the decision to take her off of life support.

It was right at the beginning of my shift. I really didn't know what to do but I was allowed to leave. I stayed the night with my sister, lying next to her in her bed as she took her last breath. My wife had been monitoring her throughout the night, comforting her as she went through her transition.

It was bittersweet for me, because although I miss my sister, I was happy that God spared her any further grief. I called her funeral a day of celebration and liberation.

Now I am the CEO and president of Heal Through Laughter, my own nonprofit under 501(c)(3), dealing with the issues of bullying, racism, violence of all kinds, the elderly, the military, or any issue where laughter can assist in the healing process. We are also producing a Healing Of A Nation Peace Tour, where we bridge the gap between law enforcement and the citizens of the inner city communities nationwide.

My wife and I are still hanging in there. I'm trying to be a better man, father, husband, and friend. It gets difficult sometimes, especally when you've spent most of your life underachieving.

Sometimes I still exhibit some of my old ways but I'm always willing to improve. It doesn't matter how old you get, you never stop learning, and as long as you recognize this your life will steadily improve.

To the Kids:

While you are young, get everything you can get. Don't waste valuable time that you will never get back on things that won't account for anything. Mind your parents and don't grow up before your time.

If you do the things I'm instructing, you will have few regrets when you get older. Be the one who tells the story of a good life, where you did everything you were supposed to do. You can be anything you want to be in life if you just believe in yourself and make the correct decisions on everything that you do.

To the Parents:

Love your children and make sure you communicate with them. Don't leave the responsibility of growing up solely on them. Provide a loving household and guide them by what you do and not what you tell them. Be patient with your children and remember to listen to them. If your child feels you are incapable of hearing what they are saying, they will be reluctant to tell you anything and will find an ear some place else.

Make sure your children eat right and that their hygiene is in proper order. Take them for regular doctor and dentist appointments. I know this may sound ridiculous, but you will be surprised at how many kids have never been to a dentist.

There was once a time when I had to worry about bullets and gangs, and now I have to worry about diabetes, high blood pressure, low cholesterol, and things like that.

We have to take care of ourselves, because we have to be there for our children and their children, and hopefully their children's children.

EPILOGUE

The most difficult thing about writing this book is that it's been a reminder of all of the mistakes I have made in my life. It is not easy to put yourself on display based on the mistakes you've made.

Everyone wants to be known for all of the great things they have done. I have some great friends who have done a great job raising their kids and taking care of their families. It is always a constant reminder to me of what I could have done and what I should have done, what I could have been and what I should have been.

The one great thing about writing *Growing Up Has Never Been Easy: Especially When You Make It Hard on Yourself*, is that by learning from my mistakes we can change the lives of kids and parents, opening up a dialogue where the parents and kids can connect or reconnect.

That is why so many kids lose their way: because they communicate with the wrong people. If you don't communicate with your children they will be forced to communicate with someone else.

Don't waste time, because time is something that is so short and you can't get it back. One day, I went to sleep and I was sixtenn with my entire life in front of me. When I woke up, I was in my forties, sitting in a federal prison cell wondering where all of the time had gone.

I spent the best part of my life telling myself that everything was going to be okay because I had time, because I was young—until I got old and time began to run out.

I want to apologize to all of those people I have hurt and let down. I want to make a special apology to my children, because they deserved better than what I gave them. I want to apologize to the women and the children of the women I had in my life.

In writing this book for others, it's also been a healing process for me. So, actually, this book means it is a time for celebration; it's the celebration of life. This could be a turning point for many of you. I know it has been for me.

I'm dedicating this book to my sister and my mother. They both died way too soon and they were amazing women. I wish they were here for this moment but I'm sure they are looking down on me, proud for persevering. I'm also dedicating this book to my father who himself is suffering from cancer.

I'm also dedicating this book to my wife for hanging in there with me, and to my children and grandchildren. It is truly a blessing to share this moment with them. I want to thank all of my family members and friends who have loved me through my ups and downs.

A special thank you goes to those of you who have gone out your way to assist me in my journey. I truly love you all and you have a special place in my heart. I will soon be a blessing to you as you have been a blessing to me. I know who you are and I haven't forgotten any of you.

CPSIA information can be obtained
at www.ICGtesting.com
Printed in the USA
FSOW04n1107061115
13072FS